D1143970

A STRAIGHTFORWARD GUIDE TO

BANKRUPTCY INSOLVENCY AND THE LAW

DAVID MARSH

Dyi

Straightforward Guides

ISBN 9781847163400

Printed by Berforts Press

Cover design by Bookworks Islington

Contents

Alternatives to Bankruptcy

The Process of Bankruptcy

Company Insolvencies

Introduction

This book deals with both personal bankruptcies and also company insolvencies. It also deals with alternatives to personal bankruptcy, such as Debt Relief Orders and Individual Voluntary Arrangements-recognising that bankruptcy is the last and final option.

Over the last three years, both personal bankruptcies and company insolvencies have risen to record levels, in large part to do with the economic climate, i.e. recession and also the steady rise in both personal debt and company debt over the last ten years or so, fuelled by an economic boom that has ended, as they all do, in tears. This time the end has resulted in the worst recession since the great depression of 1929.

It is predicted that in 2013 around 150,000 individuals will go bankrupt. Relatively new to the ranks are a lot of professionals, such as lawyers and judges. More people are going for IVA's (Individual Voluntary Arrangements, see Chapter 3,). Many people are opting for the recently introduced Debt Relief Orders, which are cheap to enter into (£90 as opposed to £525 plus £175 fee for personal bankruptcy) but applying only to those with less than £15,000 in unsecured credit debts and under £300 in assets (See Chapter 2). In addition, pensioners, once a negligible part of the whole picture, are increasingly having to seek relief from debt.

In part one, this very practical book offers a step-by-step guide to personal bankruptcy and also alternatives to bankruptcy such as Debt Management Plans, Individual Voluntary Arrangements, Administration Orders and Debt Relief Orders. The second part deals with company insolvencies, which are on the rise with several high street chains going under in the last year. The book starts by looking at the insolvency service and who's who in the world of bankruptcy, including the role of the official receiver.

The nature and type of advice available to people who are considering bankruptcy is covered. How to deal with creditors and also institutions such as banks is also covered along with the process of bankruptcy, costs, the hearing and the bankruptcy petition plus the interview with the Official Receiver.

Following the process of bankruptcy, the duties and restrictions imposed upon an individual are covered along with the eventual discharge from bankruptcy. The nature of debts included in the bankruptcy process are covered along with the treatment of assets.

Overall, this is a very practical book, complete with key forms used in the bankruptcy process. Any individual who is contemplating bankruptcy will benefit directly from the practical advice contained within.

Chapter 1

The Personnel Involved in Bankruptcy

The Insolvency Service

The Insolvency Service operates under a statutory framework-mainly the Insolvency Acts 1986 and 2000, the Company Directors Disqualifications Act 1986 and the Employment Rights Act 1996. There are a network of 38 Official Receiver offices throughout England and Wales. The Enforcement Directorate and headquarters are in London, Birmingham, Manchester and Edinburgh.

What the Insolvency Service does

The Insolvency Service:

- administers and investigates the affairs of bankrupts, of companies and partnerships wound up by the court, and establishes why they became solvent;
- acts as trustee/liquidator where no private sector insolvency practitioner is appointed;
- acts as nominee and supervisor in fast-track individual voluntary arrangements;
- takes forward reports of bankrupts' and directors misconduct;
- deals with the disqualification of unfit directors in all corporate failures;

- deals with bankruptcy restriction orders and undertakings;
- authorises and regulates the insolvency profession;
- assesses and pays statutory entitlement to redundancy payments when an employer cannot or will not pay its employees;
- provides banking and investment services for bankruptcy and liquidation estate funds;
- advises BIS ministers and other government departments and agencies on insolvency, redundancy and related issues;
- provides information to the public on insolvency and redundancy matters via its helpline 0845 602 9848, website, www.bis.gov.uk/insolvency, Leaflets and Redundancy Payments Helpline.

The Insolvency Service also carries out investigations into companies.

If you are thinking about going bankrupt you should contact the Insolvency Service on their helpline-addresses also contained in the back of this book.

The Official Receiver

The Official Receiver is a civil servant in the Insolvency Service and an Officer of the Court. He or she will be notified by the court of the bankruptcy or winding up order. He will then be responsible through his staff for administering the initial stage, at least, of the insolvency case. This stage includes collecting and protecting any assets and investigating the causes of the bankruptcy or winding up.

The Official Receiver's staff will contact you, either immediately if action is urgently needed or within 2 days of receiving an insolvency order or bankruptcy order. Usually they will arrange an appointment for you to attend the Official Receiver's office for an interview, normally within ten working days of receiving the order from the court. He or she will then act as your trustee in bankruptcy unless the court appoints an insolvency practitioner to take this role. Assuming that it is the Official Receiver who will be acting as your trustee, he or she will be responsible for looking after your financial affairs during your bankruptcy and also your financial affairs prior to you being made bankrupt.

If the Official Receiver does not require you to attend an interview you will be sent a questionnaire to fill in and return. See chapter three for the detailed process of bankruptcy and the steps involved.

****

Chapter 2

Alternatives to Bankruptcy

1. Debt Management Plans

A Debt Management Plan is a way of planning your debt payments over a number of years. It has similarities to an Individual Voluntary Arrangement in that it is a way of organising and paying off debt and keeping creditors at bay.

There are two types of Debt Management Plan:

1. The type where you are provided with standard letters and you are in charge of making payments. With this method you are in charge of dealing with your creditors.
2. The type where a third party contacts all your creditors. Using this method, your financial situation is illustrated by a set of papers called a common financial statement. You will be represented by a third party and given 24hr support.

Whichever way you go, the end result is to control your debts.

The debt management plans have no legal standing and are not ratified by a court, as is an Administration Order for example.

A debt management plan can provide solutions for the following:

- Those with unsecured debts that they cannot afford to pay
- Those with equity in their properties but who would rather not re-mortgage or take out a loan
- Those who do not qualify for an IVA, i.e. those with debts under £12,000
- For people who want a short term solution to debts i.e. those who are about to sell a home
- People who don't want to deal with their debts but would rather a third party take this on.

Essentially, a Debt Management Plan places your debt with a third party who deals with your debts on your behalf. Debt Management Plans are far more effective than taking out unregulated loans with very high rates of interest. It is very important to remember that debts with underlying security in them cannot be put into a plan.

Examples of unsecured borrowing

- Personal loans
- Overdrafts
- Credit cards
- Student loans
- Store cards

Secured debts are where the lender has a legal charge over some property of yours, so that if you default on payments, they can possess that property and sell it to get their money back.

Generally...

The length of time that the debt management plan runs will depend on the way it is structured. A simple approach is to divide your monthly payments into your debts and that is the number of months that the plan will run.

When organising the Plan you should concentrate on the priority of your debts. A priority debt is one which can have serious results if not paid, such as mortgage, utilities etc. Some loans may be secured against your home so these would be treated as priority. You will need to look carefully at your spending and cut down unnecessary expenditure. All of us have to do this, particularly in recession. Look to get cheaper deals on gas and electricity.

Beware that debt management companies, of which there are many, will charge a fee to carry out the planning and negotiating for you. The recession has provided the perfect opportunity for unscrupulous operators to target vulnerable people. When considering going down the road of a debt management plan you should contact a reputable operator, such as the Insolvency Service Enquiry Line on 0845 602 9848.

Structuring a Debt Management Plan

Before you approach a debt management company you will need to collect together information about your financial affairs and follow some simple steps:

- Make a complete list of all your debts-divide them into separate headings such as priority and non-priority debts.

You will need to make offers to pay off your priority debts before tackling non-priority debts.

- The next step is to work out your income and expenditure. Be honest and make sure the amounts are realistic. What you are trying to do here is to gain a clear picture of your situation-which can be very beneficial.

- Contact your creditors and inform them that you are putting together a debt management plan.

- Do not borrow extra money to pay off your debts. Think about ways in which you can maximise your income-for example are you claiming all the benefits that you are entitled to.

If you are managing the debt management plan yourself, it is very important that you inform your creditors that you are structuring your debt. They should then be on your side. However, as debt management plans have no legal standing, creditors do not have to accept them although, if it comes to court action against you then the fact that you have a plan will stand in your favour. Creditors are not allowed to harass you and if you are being harassed then you should contact an advice an agency, such as the Citizens Advice Bureau.

It is important, once you have structured your plan, that you let your creditors have a copy so they can see what you are doing and, hopefully, agree to it.

Making payments

Most people will pay their debt management plans by standing order through their bank account. However, it is up to the client of the company how they choose to pay, as long as it is paid in full and on time.

If you are thinking of using a debt management company, you should be aware of the following before making your decision:

- Debt management organisations will only be interested in individuals who have some income and can service their debts over time in full-and who own their own home, so that the home can be used as surety against the debts.

- Many debt management organisations will deal only with non-priority debts and leave the individual to deal with priority debts themselves.

- Most debt management companies will charge a fee, typically between £200-250 which leaves less money to pay off the debts. They might also charge a deposit at the outset.

- Most debt management companies also charge a fee to the individual each month, an administration fee. This can be quite high. Remember these companies are in business and you are their product.

- You need to check the contract that you will have with the company and that you can cancel any time if you are not happy.

- Debt Management Plans have no legal standing.

Debt management Plans and Credit status

If you are heavily in debt then this is noted on your credit reference file. By entering into a plan with a debt management company, your debts will be cleared based on agreement with creditors. After the agreed payment period is over then your credit status will begin to improve. Negative entries stay on file for six years.

Chapter 3

Alternatives to Bankruptcy
2. Individual Voluntary Arrangements

An Individual Voluntary Arrangement (IVA) is a formal agreement between you and your creditors where you will come to an arrangement with people you owe money to, which will enable you to make reduced payments towards the total amount of your debt in order to pay off a percentage of what you owe then generally after 5 years your debt is classed as settled.

Due to its formal nature, an IVA has to be set up by a licensed professional. You should first go to the official insolvency website www.insolvencyhelpline.co.uk or phone the UK Insolvency Helpline for more information (0845 602 9848) to source a licensed Insolvency Practitioner. Many firms have jumped on the insolvency bandwagon in the last few years. However, unlike these firms, the Licensed Insolvency Practitioners on the panel do not charge any fees up front for putting together a client's proposals for an Individual Voluntary Arrangement.

How IVA's work

Once a Licensed Insolvency Practitioner has made a decision that an IVA is the correct instrument for you to solve your debt problems, you will then be asked questions regarding your current financial situation. This is an in-depth interview, and, based on the information that you give, a debt repayment plan will be drawn up.

To qualify for an IVA one or more of the following criteria must apply to your situation:

- You must have debts of £12,000 or more

- The bulk of your debts must be unsecured

- You must have a regular income

- You are presently employed

- You can supply verification of income

Based on this information, with an assessment of income and outgoings a plan can be drawn up for you. You must scrutinise this plan and then sign it if you agree, or discuss it if you don't.

An application may then be made to court for an interim order. Once this order is in place, no creditors will be able to take legal action against you. Following the grant of this order the Nominee (Licensed Insolvency Practitioner) will circulate to the creditors the following information:

- The Nominee's comments on the debtor's proposals
- The proposals
- Notice of the date and location of the meeting of creditors to vote on the proposals

- A statement of affairs-this effectively being a list of the assets and the liabilities of the debtor
- A schedule advising creditors of the requisite majority required to approve the IVA
- A complete list of creditors
- A guide to the fees charged following the approval of the IVA
- A form of proxy for voting purposes

A creditor meeting will then take place at which you should attend.

For an IVA to be approved, creditors will be called on to vote either for or against the arrangement. If only one creditor votes "for" the IVA, the IVA will be approved. However, if only one creditor votes against the IVA, and they represent less than 25% of your total debt, the meeting will be suspended until a later date, and other creditors who did not vote will be called on to vote.

If the creditor who voted against the IVA represents more than 25% of the total debt you owe then the IVA will fail. This is because an IVA will only ever be approved if 75% in monetary value is voted for. If any of the creditor's don't vote it is assumed that they will vote for the IVA.

The IVA will be legally binding. As long as you keep up the repayments, when the term of your agreement is finished, you will be free from these debts regardless of how much has been paid off. During the period of the arrangement your financial situation will be reviewed regularly to see if there are any changes in your circumstances.

It is worth noting that if you do enter into an IVA with your creditors and have an endowment policy linked to your mortgage, or equity in your property or a pension fund then these will be taken into account when working out income/assets/outgoings.

Key components for a successful IVA

- The IVA must offer a higher return to creditors than could otherwise be expected were the debtor to be made bankrupt.

- An honest declaration of your assets and/or anticipated future earnings should be made. Material or false declarations are very likely to result in an unsuccessful IVA.

Advantages of an IVA

Individual, partner or sole trader

- No restrictions in regards to personal credit although in practice can be hard to obtain.

- The proposals are drawn up by the debtor and are entirely flexible to accommodate personal circumstances.

- The debtor does not suffer the restrictions imposed by bankruptcy, such as not being able to operate as a director of a limited company etc.

- The costs of administering an IVA are considerably lower than in bankruptcy, enabling a higher return to creditors.

- IVA's operate as an insolvency procedure and creditors can as a consequence of this, still reclaim tax and VAT relief as a bad debt.

- Enables a sole trader or partner to continue to trade and generate income towards repayment to creditors.

Disadvantages of an IVA

- Where contributions from income are being made, IVA's are generally expected to be for a period longer than bankruptcy, i.e. 5 years as opposed to 1 year.

- If the debtor fails to comply with the terms of the arrangement his home and assets can still be at risk if they have not been specifically excluded from the proposals.

- If the IVA fails as a consequence of the debtor not meeting obligations, it is likely that the debtor will be made bankrupt at this time.

- There will be no opportunity for a trustee in bankruptcy to investigate the actions of the debtor or possibility of hidden assets.

Chapter 4

Alternatives to Bankruptcy

3. Administration Orders

An Administration Order is a single county court order that covers all eligible debts and rolls them up together. A single payment is made every month into the court. The court staff then divides the payment up amongst creditors on a pro-rata basis. Like other court orders, an Administration Order stops creditors from taking further or separate action against you.

Rolling up your eligible debts into an administration order can save you a lot of time and also stress as the court will deal with your debts on your behalf. Any interest and other charges that were being added onto your debts are automatically stopped on the granting of an Administration Order.

There is no initial up-front fee for an Administration Order. The court takes a fee of 10 pence out of every pound owed, which means that the handling fee is 10% of your overall debts. The fee is deducted from payments into court. If you apply for a composition order at the same time that you apply for the Administration Order then the amount of time that you make payments for is limited, usually to three years. This is because, if you are paying only a very small amount to your creditors then the order could go on for years. A Composition Order is a way of making sure that this does not happen. If the judge does decide to make a Composition Order then this is usually limited to three years, meaning that you will have to pay off part of your debts only.

If you do not have a Composition Order in place, you can apply for one separately even after your Administration Order is in effect. This can be applied for using form N244.

Who is eligible to apply for an Administration Order?

You can get an Administration order if:

- You have at least two debts.

- Have at least one county court or High Court Judgement against you.

- The total of your debts is less than £5,000.

If you are seeking an Administration Order you can apply on form N92, obtainable online or from your local county court. The form has notes to help you in the completion. The first page of the form will ask you to list all of your debts. It is important that this is completed thoroughly, together with any arrears on priority debts. You should not sign the form at this stage. You need to take it to the county court and sign the declaration in front of a court officer. Always keep a copy of the form.

Once the court has accepted your application, your creditors will be automatically informed that you have applied for an Administration Order. Your creditors then have 16 days in which to lodge any objections that they may have, for example, they may consider that the payments offered are too low. Your creditors can also ask the court to not include them in the Order. Certain creditors, priority creditors, will almost certainly object, such as mortgage, utilities (gas and electricity), as they will want to reach their own arrangements with you.

If no objections are received within 16 days, and the courts are happy with what you have offered, then the Administration Order will be made. The creditors can take no further action provided that you pay what you have offered on time. If there is a problem, then the order should not be refused without a court hearing. A hearing should be arranged at court for you and you should always attend, or write to the court if your reason for non-attendance is valid. Once the order is in place you make your payment to the court and not the creditors.

The Administration Order will last until the debts are paid in full, unless a Composition Order is made. Either the creditors can ask for a review of the order at any time or you can apply to amend it in the light of changing circumstances. Details of the Administration Order are recorded on credit reference files for a period of six years from the date of the order.

Debts

Most courts will expect all of your debts to be listed on the forms, including priority debts such as mortgage. You will need to state whether the debts are in joint names and list them. Joint debts can cause problems as, because there is joint liability the creditors can still go after them. If the other person also has a court order against them and debts of less than £5,000 they can still apply for a separate Administration Order.

One important point to note is that your application may be refused if the information given reveals that you haven't got enough money to pay what you have offered.

Other factors involved in applying for an Administration Order

Certain debts are treated differently to the most common debts. Council tax arrears for previous years can be included in the Administration Order but not the current years bill, unless the council has told you that you have lost the right to pay in instalments and must pay the balance in one lump sum.

Magistrate's court fines can be included in the application but the judge may leave them out. Any social fund loans and benefit overpayments are left out, as they are not ordinary debts.

No longer able to afford payments?

If you find yourself in a position where you can no longer keep up with the terms of the order then you can apply to change the amount that you pay each month. You can use a N244 form and there shouldn't be a fee. You should state that you are applying for a variation of payments you are making under your Administration Order and say why you are applying. You should attach a copy of a personal budget sheet to indicate how you have arrived at the revised figures. The meeting to discuss amendments will be with a District Judge who can make any changes needed. If you don't keep up with the payments in the order then the court can cancel or revoke the Administration Order. If this happens your creditors can then pursue you for the debts.

Administration Order paid off?

When you have paid the Order off in full you can get a Certificate of Satisfaction from the county court. There is a fee for this, currently £15. Details of your Administration Order are kept by the Registry of County Court Judgements and by credit reference agencies. These agencies will mark your file to indicate that the debt has been paid off.

If you have a Composition Order then you can still get a Certificate of Satisfaction to show that the Administration Order has been paid but individual debts will not be marked as satisfied as they have not been paid in full. However, none of the creditors on the Administration Order can take action against you either because it has been paid in full or paid the amount owed under the Composition order.

****

Chapter 5

Alternatives to Bankruptcy
4. Debt Relief Orders

Before considering going down the road of bankruptcy, there are a number of viable alternatives, one of which may suit you. These alternatives are based on a person being solvent and having enough surplus income to pay off debts, or a proportion of debts, over a specified period. In most cases, with the exceptions of Debt Management Plans, the alternatives are ratified by the courts, administered by third parties and provide relief from creditors. In addition, any surplus debts after the expiry of the order are then written off.

Debt Management Plans are somewhat different and more personal, are not legal although can be administered by a third party. We will be discussing these at the end of this chapter.

Debt Relief Orders

What is a debt Relief Order?

A debt relief order, which came into force in April 2009, is an order you can apply for if you can't afford to pay off your debts. It is granted by the Insolvency Service and is a cheaper option than going bankrupt.

You must have unsecured debts of less than £15,000 and a low income to apply for a debt relief order. It usually lasts for one year and, during that time, none of the people that you owe money to (creditors) will be able to take action against you to get their money back. At the end of the year you will be free of all the debts listed in the order. You can't apply for a debt relief order if you:

- own things of value or have savings of over £300

- Own a vehicle worth more than £1,000

- Have a private pension fund worth over £300

To apply for a debt relief order, you will need to contact an authorised advisor who will check whether or not you meet the specific conditions and then applies for the order on your behalf. Details of authorised advisors can be obtained from the Insolvency Service, the Law Society or from a Citizens Advice Bureau. The order will cost you £90 but you can pay this in instalments over six-months.

Who can apply for a debt relief order?

You can only apply for a debt relief order if you meet certain conditions. These are when:

- You have qualifying debts of £15,000 or under. These debts must be of a certain type
- You have disposable income of less than £150 per month after expenses (normal expenses). When you work out this figure you must take into account all of the money that you have coming into your household. This includes salary and

wages, any benefits, pension, contributions from other household members and any rental income.

- The assets that you own and any savings are worth less than £300. Your motor vehicle must be worth less than £1,000 unless it has been specially adapted because you have a physical disability.

- In the last three years you must have lived, had a property or carried on a business in England or Wales.

Type of debts included in a debt relief order

As explained, only certain types of debts can be included in a debt relief order. These are termed qualifying debts and include:

- Credit cards
- Overdrafts
- Loans
- Rent
- Utilities
- Telephone
- Council tax
- Benefit overpayments
- Social fund loans
- Hire purchase or conditional sale agreements
- Buy now-pay later agreements

Certain types of debts cannot be included such as:
- Court fines and confiscation orders-basically fines relating to criminal activity

- Child support and maintenance
- Student loans

Your assets

Assets are the things of value that you own. As explained above, if you own assets worth more than £300, or if you have a motor vehicle worth more than £1,000 you won't be able to apply for a debt relief order. Examples of assets that you may own include savings, vehicles, shares, antiques, and property. This is not an exhaustive list. Essentially, anything with a value can be counted as an asset.

In relation to property, if you own a property it is very unlikely that you can apply for a Debt Relief Order. The fact that you may have a mortgage on it will not matter.

If you have not reached retirement age, but have a private or occupational pension fund, then the value of the fund counts towards the £300 limit. If you have retired and are receiving payments from a pension, then this will be regarded as income rather than an asset.

When working out what is an asset, and the value of an asset, there are some items that you don't have to take into account. These include:

- Household equipment such as bedding clothing and furniture, i.e. essential items.

- Tools, books and any other item of equipment that you may use in your business

- A car which has been specially adapted because you have a physical disability and which you need to carry out your everyday activities.

- A motor vehicle worth less than £1,000.

Those ineligible for a debt relief order

A person cannot get a debt relief order if the following applies:

- Person currently bankrupt

- You have an IVA (Individual Voluntary Arrangement) or are applying for an IVA.

- Creditors have applied to make you bankrupt but the hearing hasn't yet taken place. You might still be able to apply for a debt relief order if your creditors agree.

- You have been given a bankruptcy restrictions order or undertaking.

- You have petitioned for bankruptcy but your petition has not yet been dealt with.

- You have had a Debt Relief Order in the last six years.

- You have been given a debt relief restriction order or undertaking.

555

Applying for a Debt Relief Order

Debt relief orders are administered by the Official Receiver through the Insolvency Service. However, you can only apply for a debt relief order through a third party or intermediary and not through the Insolvency Service Direct. An intermediary is usually a skilled debt advisor who has been permission to proceed with the advice and paperwork. Intermediaries can be found by going to the Citizens Advice Service website www. Citizensadvice.org.uk. You can also find intermediaries through contacting the Insolvency Service www.insolvency.gov.uk

As mentioned above the cost of applying for a debt relief order is £90, which must be paid in cash at a payzone outlet. A list of these outlets can be found at www.payzone.co.uk. The £90 can be paid in six-monthly instalments. However, the Official receiver won't consider an application until the fee has been paid in full. The fee is non-refundable. It is an offence to give false or misleading statements in your application. Once the debt relief order has been approved then you shouldn't pay any of the creditors listed in the order. Your creditors will be informed about the order and they will be prevented from taking any action. The debt relief order will be published on the Individual Insolvency Register at wwwbis.gov.uk/insolvency. The register is available to the public. Your name and address will remain on the register for 15 months.

Things not to do before applying for a DRO or during the order

There are certain things that you cannot do either before you apply for a DRO or during the life of the DRO. Mainly:

- You cannot hide, destroy or falsify any books or documents up to one year before you apply for an order and during the order period
- You must tell the Official Receiver of any changes in your circumstances that would affect the application between making the application and the order being granted
- You cannot give away or sell things for less than they are worth to help you get a debt relief order.

If you are found guilty of doing any of the above you will be committing an offence which could prevent you obtaining an order or fined or imprisoned. If you have already been granted a debt relief order then the Official Receiver can apply for a Debt Relief Restriction Order or the debt relief order might be taken away.

During the Debt Relief Order period

During the period of a Debt Relief Order you won't have to pay towards the debts listed in the order. The creditors of these debts cannot take any action against you. A Debt Relief Order normally lasts 12 months.

However, as listed above there are certain debts that can't be included in a DRO. These include normal household expenses. You will also have to pay off any debts that are not included in the order. New debts cannot be added once an order is made. You have to tell the Official Receiver about any new debts incurred or if you have forgotten to include any new debts in the order.

Your debt relief order will appear on your credit file and remain on there for six years. This may affect your credit in the future and you might find it difficult to open a bank account.

With a Debt Relief Order in place, there are certain things that you cannot do. These are called 'restrictions' and include the following:

- Getting credit over £500 without telling the lender you have a DRO
- Carrying on a business in a different name from the one under which you were given a DRO
- Being involved with promoting, managing or setting up a limited company, without permission from court.

If the Official Receiver believes that you have provided wrong information or have been dishonest they can apply for a Debt Relief Restriction Order. If you are given a Debt Relief Restriction Order, this means that the restrictions on the things that you can do can last from 2-15 years. However, the DRO will still end 12 months after being granted and you won't have to pay off any debts listed in the order. If you don't follow the restrictions you will be committing an offence.

Changes in circumstances

You have the responsibility to inform the Official Receiver of any changes in your circumstances during the period of the DRO. This includes any assets of real value that you acquire during the DRO, e.g. money that has been left you. Failure to inform the Official Receiver might mean the cancelling of your DRO and you will then be responsible for all debts listed in the DRO.

THE PROCESS OF BANKRUPTCY

Chapter 6

The Process of Bankruptcy

Bankruptcy is one way of dealing with debts that you can no longer pay. The bankruptcy proceedings free you from debts which have simply become overwhelming and enable you to make a fresh start, subject to some restrictions outlined later. The process of bankruptcy also makes sure that your assets are shared out fairly between your creditors.

If you have decided that any of the alternatives to bankruptcy outlined in the previous chapters are not for you, and that bankruptcy is your only option, you need to be clear about the process of bankruptcy and what this entails and also the impact that it will have on the next few years following bankruptcy.

Costs of bankruptcy

It is ironic, but it is quite expensive to go bankrupt. In straitened time, this is probably the last thing that an individual needs but there is no escaping the fees. There is, however, the possibility of the courts waiving the fees in certain circumstances, e.g. if you are on income support. It is worth asking the staff at the court whether you are eligible for either waived or reduced fees.

The court fee which has to be sent in with the debtor's petition is currently £150. There is a £450 deposit towards administering your bankruptcy which must be paid in all cases. In the county court there is the need to swear an affidavit as part of the statement of affairs. This is free if sworn in the county court. However, if your bankruptcy hearing is taking place in the High Court then there is a fee of £7 to swear the affidavit. If you are married and both you and your spouse are petitioning for bankruptcy, two sets of fees are payable. Fees can be paid by postal order, cash or by building society, bank or solicitor's cheques. Personal cheques are not accepted.

How are you made bankrupt?

A court makes a bankruptcy order only after a bankruptcy petition has been presented. It is usually either presented by yourself or by one or more creditors who are owed at least £750 by you and that amount is unsecured (creditors petition).

In order to petition for your own bankruptcy you need to complete two forms-the petition and the statement of affairs-copies of which can be obtained free of charge from your local county court. They can also be downloaded from the insolvency service website www.bis.gov.uk/insolvency

The forms, as all county court forms, are numbered, the Petition is form 6.27 of the Insolvency Rules 1986 and the Statement of Affairs is form 6.28. You are required to register to use the Online Form Service. The Insolvency Service Helpline will assist you.

Submitting forms

For online forms, you will be invited to submit them when complete. If an individual changes their mind when the forms are complete then no further action needs to be taken. The forms remain in the system for six months after which they are deleted if no bankruptcy order has been made.

With the actual physical forms you need to take these with you when presenting your petition at court.

Creditor's petition

As stated above, a creditor who is owed over £750 can petition the court for your bankruptcy on the grounds that you cannot afford to pay your debts. The creditor must first serve you with a statutory demand for the money due. If the debt has not been paid or a settlement reached within twenty-one days of the demand then the courts will regard you as being unable to pay your debt and will grant a bankruptcy order.

Where is the bankruptcy order made?

Bankruptcy petitions are usually presented at the High Court in London or at a county court near to where you live, or have traded, within the last six months. A petition can be presented against you even if you are not present in England or Wales at the time. A petition can be brought in circumstances where you are out of the country but have had residential or business connections in England or Wales within the previous three years. Where a government department begins bankruptcy proceedings against you these may begin in the High Court in London or in one of the District registries. However, if you have not lived or traded in London then your case will usually be transferred to the appropriate local county court.

You can get addresses of local county courts from Her Majesty's Court Service Website www.hmcourts-service.gov.uk.

If you are presenting your petition at the county court you will need to take three copies of the completed forms with you on the day of your hearing. If you are dealing with the High Court only one set is needed.

The hearing

On the day of your hearing, the court judge has four different options which he or she may exercise, based on the particular circumstances of your case:

- Stay the proceedings, i.e. delay them if further information is needed before a bankruptcy order can be decided upon.

- Dismiss the petition-this may be because an alternative order such as an administration order will be appropriate.

- Appoint an insolvency practitioner, if it is believed that an IVA is more appropriate.

- Make a bankruptcy order. You will become bankrupt immediately on the making of the order.

The interview may not necessarily be with the judge, it could be with a clerk of the court or the judge may have already decide that a bankruptcy order will be made and the clerk will inform you of this.

After the order has been made you may be shown to an open-plan office where you will be required to speak to the Official Receiver's office, if it is deemed necessary, usually because you have assets that require dealing with immediately. Either a telephone interview will be booked or a time for a face-to-face interview will be booked.

In all other cases the court will inform the Official Receiver that a bankruptcy order has been made. He or she will then act as your trustee in bankruptcy unless the court appoints an insolvency practitioner to act for you.

Assuming that it is the Official Receiver who will be acting as your trustee, he or she will be looking after your financial affairs during your bankruptcy and also your financial affairs prior to being made bankrupt. The Official Receiver must also report to the court any matters which indicate that you may have committed criminal offences in connection with your bankruptcy.

A Member of staff from the Official Receiver's Office will contact you within two working days of receiving notice from the court. You may be asked to attend the Official Receiver's office for an interview, normally within ten working days of the order being received. Alternatively, the Official Receiver can suggest a telephone interview, again normally within ten working days of receiving the order. Telephone interviews are normally carried out where you have presented your own petition for bankruptcy, when you have not recently traded, if you have not previously been made bankrupt and where a telephone number for you is available.

Whether you are interviewed personally or by telephone you will receive a letter setting out what is required from you and you may also have to complete a questionnaire.

If a telephone interview has been arranged, the questionnaire will need to be returned by a certain date prior to the interview. If you are being interviewed in person you should take it with you.

You will need to collect together all of your financial records, paperwork generally and any other information that you need for the interview. The following will be needed:

- Financial papers, for example letters, bank statements, bank records, hire purchase agreements, credit card statements and so on.

- The last set of accounts if self-employed.

- You will need to have these available in front of you if you are interviewed by telephone.

- If you are being interviewed in person, you should take the completed questionnaire and the financial records, paperwork and any other information to the interview.

The interview in person

A face-to-face interview will take place in a private room and can last up to 2-3 hours. The questionnaire that you have filled in will be checked and if you have not filled it in you will have to do it then and there. You will then be interviewed by an examiner, a member of staff who is a specialist in insolvency matters, who will go into the details of your assets and debts and the facts and circumstances that led to bankruptcy.

You will be required to hand over all your financial records and papers. They will be examined and recorded then or at a later interview. You should ask any questions about the proceedings or the case when you are at the interview.

Telephone interviews

Telephone interviews are usually much shorter, often lasting little more than half an hour. If you have been offered and have accepted a telephone interview you will be telephoned by the examiner at the agreed time and date. The examiner will start by examining the information in the questionnaire (if you have been asked to complete one) and then will ask you for any necessary additional information about your assets and debts, and the facts and circumstances that led to your bankruptcy. You may be asked to attend another appointment, particularly if:

- The Official Receiver needs more time to complete enquiries into your or your company affairs.
- You cannot, or do not, provide all the financial records requested by the Official Receiver.
- They require more details of your assets, debts and financial affairs
- You cannot provide all the information that is needed.

There are certain assets that the Official Receiver will let you keep:

- Tools, books, vehicles and other items of equipment which you need to use personally in your employment, business or vocation.
- Clothing, bedding, furniture, household equipment and other basic items that you and your family need in your home.

You will be able to keep these items unless they can be replaced with a suitable cheaper alternative.

The trustee may apply to the court for an order restoring property to him or her if you disposed of it in a way which is unfair to your creditors (for example, if before bankruptcy you had transferred property to a relative for less than its worth). The trustee may claim property which you obtain or which passes to you (for example under a will) while you are bankrupt.

If you have made a claim against another person through court proceedings, or you think you may have a claim (a right of action) against another person, the claim may be an asset in the bankruptcy.

After the interview, either in person or by telephone, the Official Receiver will check the information you have given and based on this will issue a report to creditors setting out your assets and debts. This report will usually be issued within eight to twelve weeks of the bankruptcy order being made and the Official Receiver will begin the task of selling any assets that you might have to settle part or all of your outstanding debts. Depending on the type of assets this may take time.

Creditors

After you have been made bankrupt, creditors cannot ask you directly for money. They have to make a claim directly to the trustee. There are some very limited exceptions to this rule:

- Secured creditors, such as creditors who have a mortgage or charge on your home.
- Non-provable debts, such as court fines and other obligations arising under an order made in family proceedings or under a maintenance assessment made under the Child Support Act 1991. Non-provable debts are not included in the bankruptcy proceedings and you are still liable to pay off these debts.
- Benefit overpayments, where the benefit provider can recover any benefit overpayments from further benefits that you receive until you are discharged, when you will be released from these debts.
- Student loans

Payments to creditors

The Official Receiver will tell your creditors that you are bankrupt. He or she may either act as the trustee or may arrange a meeting of creditors for them to choose an insolvency practitioner for them to be trustee. This happens if you appear to have significant assets. You may have to attend the meeting of creditors.

The trustee will tell the creditors how much (if any) money will be shared out in the bankruptcy. Creditors will then have to make their formal claims. The costs of the bankruptcy proceedings are paid first out of any money that is available. Preferential debts are paid first, such as claims by employees (if any) together with interest on all debts. Then the other creditors are paid as far as there are funds available from the sale of your assets. If there is a surplus it will be returned to you. You would then be able to apply to the court for your bankruptcy order to be annulled.

If your trustee makes a payment to your creditors, they may place an advertisement about your bankruptcy in a newspaper asking creditors to submit their claims. Depending on how long it takes your trustee to deal with your assets, this advertisement may appear several years after the bankruptcy order.

If you have provided all the necessary information and dealing with your assets is straightforward you may not hear from the Official Receiver again. If you do not co-operate with the Official receiver's staff, you may have to attend court to be questioned and could even be arrested if you fail to co-operate. You could also have your discharge from bankruptcy proceedings suspended, which would mean that your bankruptcy could last longer than the normal twelve months.

Annulment and the Fast Track Voluntary Arrangement

Annulment of bankruptcy is a procedure whereby a court will cancel the bankruptcy order. An individual can apply to the court for an order of annulment at any time where:

- The bankruptcy order should not have been made, for example because the due process wasn't followed.

- All of your bankruptcy debts and fees and expenses of the bankruptcy have been paid in full or guaranteed to the court.

- You have agreed an IVA with your creditors to repay all or part of your debts.

An annulment means that, legally, a bankruptcy order was never made and you will revert to your status before bankruptcy. However, any disposals of your property by the trustee will be valid and cannot be reversed. Any assets remaining will be returned to you and you will be liable for any debts that have not been paid in the bankruptcy.

Fast Track Voluntary Arrangement

If you have been made bankrupt by one of your creditors but think that you can provide a significantly better return to your creditors than they will receive through your bankruptcy, then by entering into a Fast Track Voluntary Arrangement (FTVA) you can get your bankruptcy annulled.

An FTVA is a binding agreement made between you and your creditors to pay all or part of the money you owe. It can only be entered into after you have been made bankrupt. In order to enter into a FTVA you must secure the co-operation of the Official Receiver, who will act as your nominee. They will help you put together your proposal for your creditors.

For the FTVA to be accepted, 75% of the creditors who vote must agree to the proposal. It is then legally binding, and no creditor can take legal action regarding the debt provided you keep to the agreement. As nominee, the Official Receiver will then supervise the arrangement, making payment to your creditors in accordance with your proposals.

Costs of the FTVA

The fee for acting as nominee is £310. Additionally, for carrying out the ongoing role of supervisor of the FTVA the Official Receiver will charge fifteen per cent of monies from any assets you own or any money collected from you. You will also be required to pay a £10 registration fee for your FTVA to be recorded on the public register of individual voluntary arrangements.

Duration of the FTVA

There is no fixed period for a FTVA. It lasts as long as is agreed and will be outline in the proposal. Once the FTVA has been agreed the Official Receiver will apply to have your bankruptcy annulled, as if it never existed. You will no longer be subject to the restrictions in the bankruptcy order. However, if you fail to comply with the order then the Official Receiver will make you bankrupt again. If the circumstances are beyond your control, such as being made redundant then the Official Receiver will take no action against you. However, your creditors can once again petition for your bankruptcy.

Amending records

Individual Insolvency Register-this will be amended on annulment. It will be your responsibility to have details of your bankruptcy order removed from your credit file. The Official

Receiver will also inform anyone who has been informed of the bankruptcy order that the order is now annulled.

Generally...

Your home

If you own your home, whether freehold or leasehold, solely or jointly, mortgaged or other wise, your interest in the home will form part of your estate which will be dealt with by the trustee. The home may have to be sold to go towards paying your debts.

If your spouse and/or children are living with you, it may be possible for the sale of the property to be put off until after the end of the first year of your bankruptcy. This gives time for other housing arrangements to be made. Your husband, wife/partner, relative or friend may be able to buy your interest in your home from the trustee. If the trustee cannot, for the time being, sell your property he or she may obtain a charging order on your interest in it, but only if that interest is worth more than £1,000. If a charging order is obtained, your interest in the property will be returned to you, but the legal charge over your interest will remain. The amount covered by the legal charge will be the total value of your interest in the property and this sum must be paid from your share of the proceeds when you sell the property.

Until your interest in the property is sold, or until the trustee obtains a charging order over it, that interest will continue to belong to the trustee but only for a certain period, usually only 3 years, and will include any increase in its value. The benefit of any increase in value will go to the trustee to pay debts, even if the home is sold some time after you have been discharged from bankruptcy.

Pension rights

A trustee cannot claim a pension as an asset if your bankruptcy petition was presented on or after May 29th 2000, as long as the pension scheme has been approved by HM Revenue and Customs. For petitions presented before May 29th 2000, trustees can claim some kind of pensions. However, given that we are now in 2010, this is not so relevant. Generally, the trustee will be able to claim any interest that you have in a life assurance policy. The trustee may be entitled to sell or surrender the policy and collect any proceeds on behalf of your creditors. If the policy is held in joint names, for instance with your husband or wife, that other person is likely to have an interest in the policy and should contact the trustee immediately to discuss how their interest in the policy should be dealt with.

Your life insurance policy

You may want a life insurance policy to be kept going. You should ask the trustee about this. It may be possible for your interest to be transferred for an amount equivalent to the present value of that interest.

If the life insurance policy has been legally charged to any person, for instance an endowment policy used as security for your mortgage, the rights of the secured creditor will not be affected by the making of the bankruptcy order. But any remaining value in the policy may belong to the trustee.

Your wages

Your trustee may apply to court for an Income Payments Order (IPO) which requires you to make contributions towards the bankruptcy debts from your income. The court will not make an IPO if it would leave you without enough income to meet the reasonable needs of you and your family. The IPO can be increased or decreased to reflect any changes in income.

IPO payments continue for a maximum of 3 years from the date of the order and may continue after you have been discharged from bankruptcy. Or you may enter into a written agreement with your trustee, called an Income Payments Agreement (IPA), to pay a certain amount of your income to the trustee for an agreed period, which cannot be longer than 3 years. Each case is assessed individually.

Restrictions on a bankrupt

The following are criminal offences for an un-discharged bankrupt:

- Obtaining credit of £500 or more either alone or jointly with any other person without disclosing your bankruptcy. This is not just borrowed money but any kind of credit whatsoever.
- Carrying on business (directly or indirectly) in a different name from that in which you were made bankrupt, without telling all of those with whom you are doing business the name in which you were made bankrupt.

- Being concerned (directly or indirectly) in promoting, forming or managing a limited company, or acting as a company director, without the court's permission, whether formally appointed as a director or not.

You may not hold certain public offices. You may not hold office as a trustee of a charity or a pension fund. After the bankruptcy order, you may open a new bank account but you should tell them that you are bankrupt. They may impose conditions and limitations. You should ensure that you do not obtain overdraft facilities without informing the bank that you are bankrupt, or write cheques that are likely to be dishonoured.

Ending bankruptcy

If you were made bankrupt on or after April 1st 2004, you will automatically be freed from bankruptcy after a maximum of twelve months. This period may be shorter if the Official receiver concludes his enquiries into your affairs and files a notice in court. You will also become free from bankruptcy immediately if the court cancels the bankruptcy order. This would normally happen when your debts and fees and expenses of the bankruptcy proceedings have been paid in full, or the bankruptcy order should not have been made.

On the other hand, if you have not carried out your duties under the bankruptcy proceedings, the Official Receiver or your trustee may apply to the court for the discharge to be postponed. If the court agrees, your bankruptcy will only end when the suspension has been lifted and the time remaining on your bankruptcy period has run.

Debts

Discharge releases you from most of the debts you owed at the date of the bankruptcy order. Exceptions include debts arising from fraud and any claims which cannot be made in the bankruptcy itself. You will only be released from a liability to pay damages for personal injuries to any person if the court see fit.

When you are discharged you can borrow money and carry on business without these restrictions. You can act as a company director, unless disqualified.

Assets that you obtained or owned before your discharge

When you are discharged there may still be assets that you owned, either when your bankruptcy began, or which you obtained before your discharge, which the trustee has not yet dealt with. Examples of these may be an interest in your home, an assurance policy or an inheritance.

These assets are still controlled by the trustee who can deal with them at any time in the future. This may not be for a number of years after your discharge.

Assets you obtain after your discharge

Usually, you may keep all assets after your discharge.

Bankruptcy restriction orders and undertakings

If, during the enquiries into your affairs, the Official Receiver decides that you have been dishonest either before or during the bankruptcy, or that you are otherwise to blame for your position, they may apply to the court for a Bankruptcy Restrictions Order.

The court may make an order against you for between 2-15 years and this order will mean that you continue to be subject to the restrictions or bankruptcy. You may give a bankruptcy restrictions undertaking which will have the same effect as an order, but will mean that the matter does not go to court.

Debts incurred after you have been made bankrupt

Bankruptcy deals with your debts at the time of the bankruptcy order. After that date you should manage your finances a lot more carefully. New debts can result in a further bankruptcy order or prosecution.

Credit reference agencies

After you have been discharged from bankruptcy, you will want to ensure that you have a clear idea of your credit rating and also that the details that the credit agencies hold on you is correct. The three main consumer credit reference agencies in the UK are Experian, Equifax and Call Credit. They provide lenders with information about potential borrowers which in turn enables the lenders to make their decisions. The agencies hold information about most adults in the UK. However, sometimes this information is out of date, or incorrect in other ways which can adversely affect your credit.

If personal information about you is incorrect or out of date you have the right to change it under the Data Protection Act 1988. You can ask for a copy of your credit report inline or by post from a credit reference agency for £2. You need to provide your name, and any previous name such as maiden name, address and any addresses lived in for the last six years and your date of birth. The credit reference agency must provide you with details within seven working days. The addresses and contact details of each agency are as follows:

Experian 0844 481 8000 www.experian.co.uk

Equifax 0870 010 0583 www.equifax.co.uk

Call Credit 0870 060 1414 www.callcredit.co.uk

Checking the information on your credit file

A bankruptcy will stay on your credit file for six years from the date of your bankruptcy order. You should ensure that the date of your discharge from bankruptcy is correctly shown. If it is not, you should send your certificate of discharge to the agency as proof. Alternatively, a letter of discharge can be obtained from the Official receiver.

Accounts included in your bankruptcy order may show on your credit report as being in default. The date of the default should be no later than the bankruptcy order.

Making a complaint

If the credit reference agency still does not amend the problem after you have contacted them then you can write to the Information Commissioner, who has responsibility for enforcing the Data Protection Act. You should write giving all details of yourself and the problem and they will decide on the action to take. The Information Commissioners Office can be contacted on 0845 630 6060.

Website www.ico.gov.uk

You can, if you so wish use credit repair companies who will, for a fee, undertake checking and rectification of your credit rating.

Company Insolvency

Chapter 7

Compulsory Liquidation

___

Company insolvency generally

Insolvency proceedings are formal measures taken to deal with company debt. As will be outlined, there are many different types of insolvency proceedings.

In the following chapters we cover Compulsory Liquidation, Members Voluntary Liquidation, Creditors Voluntary Liquidation, Administration and Company Voluntary Arrangements. We also cover estates of deceased persons and insolvent partnerships.

The chapters covering compulsory winding-up and receivers apply to both registered and unregistered companies whilst voluntary winding up and administration applies to registered companies only

What is liquidation?

Liquidation is a legal process in which a liquidator is appointed to 'wind up' the affairs of a limited company. At the end of the process, the company ceases to exist. Liquidation does not mean that the creditors of a company will get paid. In many cases it means the opposite. The main purpose of liquidation is to ensure that all of the company's affairs have been dealt with properly. This involves:

- ensuring all company contracts (including employee contracts) are completed, transferred or brought to an end;
- ceasing the company's business;
- settling any legal disputes;
- selling any assets;
- collecting in money owed to the company; and
- distributing any funds to creditors and returning share capital to the shareholders (after repayment of debts)

When it is done the liquidator will apply to have the company removed from the register at Companies House and dissolved.

The supervision of insolvency procedures

All liquidators, administrators, administrative receivers and supervisors must be authorised insolvency practitioners. Receiver managers, Law of Property Act receivers and nominees appointed to manage a corporate voluntary arrangement moratorium do not have to be authorised. Insolvency practitioners may be authorised by a number of different bodies. A list of these bodies can be found on the Insolvency Service website listed further on in this book.

Compulsory liquidation

The High Court alone has jurisdiction in winding up proceedings if the issued share capital of a company is in excess of £120,000. Proceedings can either be commenced in the

Companies Court in London or at one of the eight provincial district registries with chancery jurisdiction. Enquiries can be made of a central register to see whether a winding up petition is pending. The county court in the district in which the company is operating also has jurisdiction in winding up proceedings if the share capital does not exceed £120,000. In London, no county courts have bankruptcy jurisdiction. If the petition is presented in the wrong court, the court can transfer the proceedings or allow the proceedings to continue where they are, providing the court has winding up jurisdiction. The court can also strike out proceedings.

Preparing and serving the statutory demand

Like the demand served on an individual, a statutory demand served on a company is in prescribed form requiring the debtor to pay the debt contained within the demand or secure or compound the debt to the creditors satisfaction within the period of three weeks after the demand has been served.

The demand must exceed £750, its purpose to show that the company cannot meet its liabilities. The demand can be from one or more persons. The form of statutory demand is prescribed by schedule 4 to the rules , form 4.1. This form can be obtained from your local court or the Insolvency Service website www.bis.gov.uk/insolvency. A petition can also be based on an unsatisfied execution or on the inability of the company to pay debts-in which there is no minimum debt requirement. The demand must be left at the registered office of the company. Service by post is not available unless the debtor-company acknowledges that the demand was received.

Creditors petition

The petition must be presented to either the High court or to the appropriate county court. In London this is:

The High Court
Royal Courts of Justice
Companies Court
Strand
London WC2A 2LL
Tel: 020 7947 6000

Any District Registry of the High Court

In a county court where the following applies:

- the county court deals with insolvency matters; and
- the county court covers the area where the company's trading address or registered office is situated; and
- the paid up share capital of the company is £120,000 or less.

A company is deemed unable to pay its debts if a creditor has served a statutory demand for the minimum amount and the company has neglected to pay the sum or to secure or compound it within three weeks after service of the demand. If the execution or other process against the company is returned unsatisfied in whole or in part (no minimum debt requirement), then a company is also deemed to be unable to pay its debts,

A company is also deemed unable to pay its debts if its liabilities exceed its assets. A Statutory demand does not have to have been served on a company for a petition to be presented for its winding up. If the debt is due and unpaid, and cannot be disputed on a substantial ground, then this is evidence that there is an inability to pay.

There is a prescribed form of petition (form 4.2) set out in schedule 4 to rules. (see below for filling out the petition). This form can be obtained from the Insolvency Service website.

If two or more creditors are jointly petitioning, all their details must be given. Secured creditors must value their security and can only petition for the unsecured part of their debt. The petition must state the amount of the debt and the consideration for it. Every petition must be verified by an affidavit. The affidavit must exhibit a copy of the petition.

Completing the petition
Paragraphs 1-4

You will need to make a search at Companies House, 21 Bloomsbury Street, London WC1B 3XD in person or by telephone on 0303 1234 500 or on-line at www.companieshouse.gov.uk

Paragraph5

You must state the grounds for winding up. This will typically mean including details about debt. In all cases, you should state that the company has not paid the debt, or a specified part of it, and that you believe the company is insolvent and unable to pay its debt.

Paragraph7

You need to state whether the EC Regulation on Insolvency Proceedings 2000 does or does not apply, If the EC Regulation does apply. You need to state whether the proceedings will be `main' `secondary' or `territorial'. If the company is registered in England and Wales and mainly carries on business in England and Wales, the EC Regulation will apply and the proceedings will be main proceedings. In other circumstances you should seek advice.

Paragraph 8

If the company has been dissolved you will need to ask the court to restore the company to the Register of Companies before making the winding up order. To do this, you add an extra clause to the `prayer' saying that the company name should be restored to the register. Further information on the restoration of companies is available from the Treasury Solicitors website at www.bonavacantia.gov.uk

On the issue of a petition, the following are required:

- petition together with copies for service on the company and any other party, such as administrator, administrative receiver, supervisor or voluntary liquidator
- affidavit verifying the petition
- receipt for the deposit payable to the official receiver (currently £1,165 as at 2012)
- The fee (currently £220 as at 2012)

All copies of the petition are sealed by the court except for one, and handed back to the petitioner. The petition is endorsed with time date and place of the court hearing. At least one director of the company must receive a sealed copy or a person authorised to receive it. It can be left at the registered office. If none of these methods of service are utilised, or can be utilised, then the court may allow substituted service on an ex-parte application. If a voluntary arrangement is in force, the supervisor must be served as well as the company unless it is the supervisor who is petitioning. If an administrative receiver has been appointed, that person must also be served if the company is already in voluntary liquidation, the voluntary liquidator must be served.

The petition must be advertised in the London Gazette not less than seven business days before the hearing and not less than seven business days after service.

The form of advertisement is prescribed (form 4.6). All creditors, directors and shareholders of the company are entitled to be furnished with a copy of the petition within two days of requesting the same on payment of a fee.

The petitioner or his solicitor must lodge a certificate showing compliance with the rules, together with the gazette advertisement, at least five business days before the hearing. Petitions are initially set down for hearing before a registrar of the company's court in London or a district judge (of the High Court or county court) elsewhere. If the petition is opposed, it must be adjourned to a High court or circuit judge.

Any creditor who intends to appear on the hearing of the petition must give notice to the petitioning creditor. The notice must states the amount of debt and whether he intends to support or oppose the petition. The petitioning creditor must prepare a list of the creditors who have given notice to appear. The courts will generally look at the list of those who oppose and support the petition and the quality of the list before making a decision. It does not automatically follow that it will be dismissed if there are opponents. If the petitioning creditor has received his monies, another creditor may be substituted for him. A petition cannot be withdrawn except for leave of the court. If a petition has been served but not advertised and the company consents, leave to withdraw will be given on an ex-parte application providing that this is applied at least five days before the hearing.

The hearing of the petition

On the hearing of the petition the court may make a winding up order, adjourn the hearing conditionally or unconditionally or dismiss the petition. The general rule is that if there are a majority of creditors in value supporting a petition, then a winding up order will be made. An order that costs of the petitioning creditor be paid out of the assets of the company will usually be made by the court. These costs are a first charge on the companies assets and rank ahead of all other claims of secured creditors (including a fixed charge).

The winding up order (form 4.11 in schedule 4) is then drafted by the court and a draft is sent to the petitioning creditor or his solicitors who will engross the draft and then return it to the court for sealing (together with sufficient copies). The court sends three sealed copies to the Official Receiver who in turn will serve a copy on the company and the Registrar of Companies and arranges for the order to be advertised. The court will also inform the Official Receiver of the making of the order immediately after it has been made. If the petition is dismissed, the court will draft the order and submit it to the petitioning creditor or his solicitor for engrossment.

Before and after a company winding up

If a company goes into liquidation, any disposition of its property (including payments made by it) after the date of presentation of the petition is void (unless made with the consent of, or subsequently ratified by, the court). Once a winding up petition has been presented, the court may stay action or other legal process against the debtor or his property. The granting of a stay is discretionary. If the proceedings are pending in the High court, that court may stay the proceedings. Otherwise application must be made to the court dealing with the winding up petition. Any attachment, distress or execution issued against the company is also void and a creditor who, prior to the date of presentation of the petition, issued an attachment or execution which remained incomplete at that date cannot retain the benefit of his action. A distraining creditor can retain the benefit of his distraint.

Once a winding up order has been made or a provisional liquidator has been appointed, no creditor of the company may commence any action against the company without leave of the court. This rule does not affect the right of a creditor to the benefit of executions completed before the presentation of the winding-up petition.

Executions are complete when goods have been sold and proceeds held by the sheriff or bailiff for at least 14 days, when a charging order absolute has been obtained or when a debt garnished has been paid. A secured creditor is not affected by these provisions and can enforce his security though he cannot take any action in connection with any unsecured shortfall.

Appointment of a provisional liquidator

If it is necessary to protect the company's property prior to the hearing of the winding up petition, the court can, on the application of the company, the petitioner or creditor, appoint the official receiver or some other fit person. The court will specify the powers that they rescind or vary any order made by it. An application to rescind must normally be made within seven days, though the court will normally extend the time for applying in appropriate cases. If the proceedings have been transferred from one court to another after the making of the winding up order, the transferee court can also exercise this power.

In all cases where a winding up order is made and later the appointment of provisional liquidator, the directors or other officers of the company are obliged to submit a statement of affairs. The statement must be submitted to the official receiver within 21 days of the making of the winding up order or the appointment of a provisional liquidator or such longer time as the court or the Official Receiver may allow.

The statement must contain full particulars of the company's creditors, debts and other liabilities and of its assets together with such information as may be prescribed. Form 4.17 (in Schedule 4 to the rules) is the prescribed form for the statement of affairs. The official receiver is obliged to give to the persons making the statement a copy of the form. The official receiver may himself employ someone to assist the deponents with the statement of affairs, paid for out of the assets of the company.

Public examination

The Official Receiver may make an application to the court for the public examination of the former officers. The Official receiver must make an application for a public examination if requested to do so by half in value of the creditors or 75% of the contributors. If the examinee fails to attend the public examination without reasonable excuse, he is guilty of contempt of court.

At the public examination, the official receiver, the liquidator, any creditor who has tendered a proof of debt or any contributory can ask questions and can with the approval of the court, appear by solicitor or counsel or authorise in writing another person to question the bankrupt on his behalf. The person being examined is entitled to legal representation. If criminal proceedings have commenced against a director and the court is of the opinion that the continuation of the examination would be likely to prejudice a fair trial of those proceedings, the examination may be adjourned.

The court may order any former officer of the company or any person thought to have information relating to the property of the company to attend court and to answer questions. If the person does not attend he can be arrested and brought before the court.

Appointing a liquidator

The Official Receiver is liquidator until someone else is appointed. A liquidator can be appointed by a general meeting of the creditors, the court or by the Secretary of State. Only an authorised insolvency practitioner can act as liquidator, The Official Receiver must decide within 12 weeks of the making of the winding up order whether or not to summon a meeting of the creditors and appoint a liquidator. 21 days notice should be given to creditors of such meeting. Notice must also be given in local newspaper and the London Gazette. The Official Receiver will act as chair of the first meeting and the liquidator at all other meetings. Resolutions are deemed to be passed on a majority in value of creditors and contributors present personally or by proxy.

There has to be a quorum present that consists of at least one creditor.

The primary purpose at the first meeting is to appoint a liquidator. No resolution can be proposed which suggests the Official Receiver as the liquidator. The Official Receiver will remain the liquidator only if another is not proposed and the Official Receiver does not ask the Secretary of State to be a liquidator insolvency practitioner.

Creditors can resolve to establish a liquidator committee but a committee cannot be established at any other time when the Official Receiver is liquidator. Any creditor other than a secured creditor is eligible to be a member of the committee. A body corporate can be a member of the committee but can only act through a representative. A creditors committee must consist of at least three and not more than five members.

The role of the committee is primarily supervisory. It determines the liquidator's remuneration. The liquidator is under a duty to report to the committee all matters of concern to it in relation to the administration of the estate. The first meeting of the committee must take place within three months of its establishment and thereafter within 21 days of a request for a meeting by a committee member. The quorum for the meeting is two. The liquidator can seek to obtain the agreement of the committee to a resolution by sending to every member a copy of the proposed resolution.

Chapter 8

Voluntary liquidation

There are two types of voluntary liquidation:

1. Members voluntary liquidation (MVL)- which means that the directors have made a statutory declaration of solvency;
2. Creditors Voluntary Liquidation (CVL) – which means that the directors have not made such a declaration.

Members Voluntary Liquidation

This can take place when the directors of a company believe that the company is solvent. A majority of the company's directors must make a statutory declaration of solvency in the 5 weeks before a resolution to wind up the company is passed.

The statutory declaration will state that the directors have made a full inquiry into the company's affairs and that, having done so, they believe that the company will be able to pay its debts in full within 12 months from the start of winding up. The declaration will include a statement of the company's assets and liabilities as at the latest practicable date before making the declaration.

The liquidation starts when the members, in general meetings, pass a resolution (Companies Act 2006) (Usually a special resolution) to wind up the company voluntarily. Notice of the special must be published in the Gazette within 14 days of the resolution with a copy sent to the Registrar.

Creditor's voluntary liquidation

When it appears to the directors that a company cannot continue to trade by reason of its insolvency, the directors can resolve to convene meetings of its shareholders and creditors to consider and, if thought fit, to pass a resolution that the company be wound up. The shareholders meeting must be convened in accordance with the memorandum and articles of association of the company and the Companies Act 2006. The creditors meeting is governed by the Insolvency Act 1986 s 98. At least seven days notice of the meeting must be given to creditors.

The meeting must be advertised in the London Gazette and local newspapers. The creditors meeting must be held not more than 14 days after the shareholders meeting, though both meetings are usually held on the same day, A list of creditors must be available for inspection in the locality where the company trade or an insolvency practitioner must be named who can provide a list of names on request.

The purpose of the meeting is to resolve to put the company into liquidation and to appoint a liquidator and a liquidation committee. If a company has already been placed in members voluntary liquidation and it appears to the liquidator that all the creditors debts will not be paid, in full or part, or within 12 months of the liquidation commencing, he must call meetings of creditors in much the same way as meeting under s 98.

It is the duty of directors to nominate one of their number to chair meetings and lay before the meeting a statement of affairs. The shareholders at the meeting not only resolve that the company proceed to voluntary liquidation but also nominate someone to act as liquidator. If the creditors at their meeting make no fresh nominations, then shareholders nominee as liquidator will be confirmed in office.

The liquidator must advertise his appointment in local newspapers and also lodge a notice of his appointment with the registrar of local companies. The liquidator can ask directors to produce accounts and can provide for the cost of preparation out of the company's assets. The liquidator is obliged to give all creditors within 28 days of meeting a copy of the statement of affairs and a report of what took place at the meeting.

Alternatives to liquidation

There are three alternatives to liquidation:

- informal arrangement- where the company decides to deal with its problems itself;
- Company Voluntary Arrangement (CVA) this is a formal version of the above arrangement dealt with through the courts;
- Administration- this is a procedure that gives the company some breathing space from any action by creditors. A company may enter administration to enable the company to survive as a going concern, for a better result to be achieved than winding up and the realisation of property for benefit of secured or preferential creditors.

The procedure is managed by an administrator, who must be an authorised insolvency practitioner and who may be appointed by the court, a floating charge holder or the company or its directors.

****

Chapter 9

All Liquidations-General

The powers of the liquidator

The Liquidator may disclaim any property of the company that is onerous. This is property that is unsaleable or may give rise to a liability to pay money or perform any other onerous task on behalf of the company. In order to disclaim the liquidator must give a notice in the prescribed form (form 4.53 in schedule 4 to the rules), file at court the notice and serve the same on the party affected. If the liquidator disclaims a lease, the court can vest the property in any person claiming an interest in that property, the guarantor of any liability in respect of the property or, in the case of a dwelling house, the occupant.

Disclaimer operates so as to determine the rights, interests and liabilities of the company in respect of a disclaimed property. Disclaimer does not affect the rights and liabilities of third parties except in so far as necessary in releasing the company from any liability. Accordingly, a guarantor of a lease disclaimed by the liquidator is released from ant further liability as from the date of the disclaimer unless the company was only an assignee of the lease.

Mutual credit and sell off

An account must be taken of what sum is due from the company to a person with whom there have been mutual credits, mutual debts or other dealings. The sum due from one party must be set off against the sum due from the other and only the balance of the account is provable in the liquidation or is to be paid to the liquidator for the benefit of all creditors. For set off to be allowed , there must be obligations on both sides giving rise to pecuniary liabilities so that an account can be taken and a balance struck. If the obligation on the one side is to deliver goods and on the other is to pay a sum of money, there can be no set off.

For set off to be successful, both liabilities must have arisen prior to the commencement of the liquidation even though one of the debts may not be immediately due and not enforceable until a time after the liquidation began. There can be no set off between separate debts and joint debts. Debts must be due in the same right. Set off will not be allowed where credit was given to the same company by a creditor who had knowledge of the calling of a creditors meeting under s98 or of the presentation of a winding up petition,

If a creditor has to pay money to a liquidator, he cannot set off against the sum he is required to pay any sum due to him from the company. Right to set off may exist even though one of the debts may be secured.

General control of the liquidator

There are many powers which the liquidator can exercise only with permission of a liquidation committee or, if there is no committee, with permission of the Secretary of State. Some powers can be exercised without sanction in a voluntary liquidation but only with sanction in a winding up by the court. These powers are set out in ss165 and 166 (voluntary liquidation) and s167 (winding up by the court) and schedule 4 as follows:

. Carrying on the business of the company
. instituting or defending any legal actions (in a winding up by the court)
. compromising any claim by company against a third party: and
. compromising any dispute with the company's creditors.

The liquidator may, without the permission of the liquidation committee, sell the company's property and borrow money on the security of the company's assets. If the liquidator does anything which requires permission but without obtaining that permission, his actions can be ratified if the committee is satisfied that he acted in a case of urgency and applied to the committee without undue delay.

The liquidator does not require the committee's sanction to employ a solicitor. He should, however, give notice of his actions to the liquidation committee. The liquidator has power to summon meetings of creditors so as to ascertain creditor's wishes. Creditors have the right to apply to court for any decision of the committee, and can call a meeting of creditors to resolve otherwise. If still not satisfied he can apply to the court.

Similarly, creditors can apply to the court to reduce liquidators charges. The liquidation committee can require the liquidator to insist that his solicitors fees be taxed notwithstanding that he is of the opinion that they are reasonable.

The liquidator is subject to control by the court on the application of any creditor or contributory. The liquidator is subject to control by the Department of Trade on the monetary aspects of his administration.

The liquidator in winding up by the court is required to pay all the monies into the insolvency account at the Bank of England within 14 days of receipt of funds. In a voluntary liquidation he must pay any monies received by him and undistributed after six months into the insolvency services account at the Bank of England.

He is also obliged to send to the Secretary of State an account of all his receipts and payments every year. The court will not allow the liquidator in a winding up by court to retain or claim monies for distribution among the creditors when it would be inconsistent with natural justice to do so and something which an honest man would not do.

Adjustment of prior transaction

The kind of matters liable to be set aside are transactions at an under-value or preferences. The liquidator has power to apply to the court for the reversal of certain transactions if they were to the disadvantage of the company and were carried out at a "relevant time". The relevant time is defined in s240 in relation to transactions at an undervalue or preference as being any time in the two years preceding the onset of insolvency but, in the case of preferences not benefiting a connected person, at any time in the period of six months prior to the onset of insolvency.

Transactions cannot be set aside if the company was able to pay its debts at the time of the events or because unable to do so as a result. A company is deemed to be unable to pay its debts if it has failed to comply with a statutory demand served on it, or has allowed execution to go unsatisfied or if its liabilities exceed its assets at any one time.

Where a company entered into a transaction at an under value at a relevant time, the court can order the return of the benefit. For an order to be made, the court must be satisfied that the company had entered into a transaction.

Where a creditor has, before the commencement of the winding up, issued execution against the goods or land of the company or attached any debt due to it, he cannot retain the benefit of his actions as against the liquidator unless execution or attachment was completed prior to the commencement of the winding up. All forms for distraint are subject to the rule that if they have taken place in the three months prior to the making of the winding up order, the proceeds of the distraint are "charged) with the preferential debt.

No lien or other right to possession of any books, papers or other records of the company is enforceable against the liquidator.

Debts and dividends

There are four classes of creditor-secured, preferential, unsecured or deferred. A secured creditor is not given any special priority by the Act or the Rules but can rely on his security. He may, with the agreement of the liquidator and leave of the court, at any time alter the value which he has, in the proof of his debt, placed on his security. Though if he petitioned for the winding up of his company or has voted in respect of his unsecured balance he may only re-value his security with leave of the court.

If a secured creditor omits to disclose his security in his proof of debt, he must surrender it for the general benefit of creditors unless the court relieves him on the ground that omission was a mistake. A liquidator may redeem the security of the value placed on it by the creditor if he so wishes and a secured creditor has the right to call on the liquidator to elect whether or not to exercise the power.

Preferential debts are defined in s386 and schedule 6 to the Act. They consist primarily of taxes such as PAYE, VAT and social security contributions. Amounts due to employees for wages for the four months prior to the making of the winding up order or resolution to wind up but not exceeding £800 for each employee are preferential, together with all arrears of holiday pay. If monies have been advanced by a third party to pay wages and holiday pay which otherwise would have been preferential debt, then the person who advanced the money becomes a preferential creditor for the amount advance. Unsecured creditors are the ordinary debts of the company which are neither secured nor preferential.

Provable debts

All claims by creditors against the company are provable in the liquidation whether they are present or future, certain or contingent, ascertained or sounding-in damages. Even un-liquidated damages of tort are provable debts.

Proofs of debts

Every person claiming to be a creditor in a winding up by the court must submit his claim in writing to the Official Receiver or the liquidator-this is called proving his debt. In voluntary liquidation, formal proofs of debts are not usually required-a claim in any form is sufficient but the liquidator can call for a formal proof of debt to be submitted. A proof of debt must be in the prescribed form (form 4.25 in schedule 4 to the rules) or a substantially similar form. Proof of debt forms must be sent out by the Official Receiver or liquidator to every creditor who is known to him or identified in the statement of affairs. The liquidator may require a proof of debt to be verified by affidavit in form 4.26. A proof of debt must contain details of the creditors name and address, the amount owing, the date of the liquidation, the date of the liquidation, whether interest and VAT is included, whether any part of the debt is preferential, how the debt was incurred and particulars of any security held and its value.

There is no time limit for submission of proofs of debt but a creditor who has not proved his debt cannot benefit from any distribution prior to proof. Before declaring a dividend, the liquidator must give notice of his intention to do so to all creditors of whom he is aware and who have not proved their debts. The notice must specify the last date for proving which must not be less than 21 days after the date of the notice and must state the liquidators intention to declare a dividend. The liquidator cannot declare a dividend until he has examined every proof of debt. If a creditor is dissatisfied at the decision of the liquidator, the court may reverse that decision.

Interest

When a debt proved in a liquidation bears interest the proof of debt can include interest up to the date of the liquidation. If the debt does not include the right to interest, interest can none the less be claimed up to the date of liquidation.

Vat

A creditor whose claim includes an element of VAT can either prove for the whole amount of the claim (and pay to HMRC the VAT element irrespective of whether or not he receives any dividend) or prove for the amount of his claim net of VAT and reclaim the VAT. No formalities are required to reclaim the VAT element of the debt owed by the bankrupt-the creditor is automatically entitled to VAT bad debt relief once he has written off the debt in his books and the debt is no more than six-months old.

Dividends

The liquidator must give notice of a dividend to all creditors who have proved their debts. The notice must include details of the amount realised from the sale of the assets, payments made by the liquidator in his administration, the total amount distributed, the rate of dividend and whether any further dividends are to be expected. The liquidator must not, except with the leave of the court, proceed to declare a dividend where there is a pending application to vary a decision of his on a proof of debt.

If the liquidator is unable to declare any or any further dividend, he must give notice to this effect to creditors. A creditor who has failed to lodge his proof of debt before an interim dividend was declared is not entitled to receive a payment in priority to other creditors from further funds available.

The liquidator cannot be sued for a dividend but if he refuses to pay a dividend the court may order him to pay it together with, out of his own funds, interest at judgement rate and costs. When the liquidator is ready to close his administration, he must give notice to creditors of his intention to declare a final dividend or that no further dividend will be declared. The notice must require any remaining claims to be established by a certain date: if they are not, they can be ignored by the liquidator.

****

Chapter 10

Receivership

Nature of receivership

There are three kinds of receivership-under the Law of Property Act in respect of a property, by the court and by a debenture holder under a floating charge debenture. Court appointed receivers are rare. If a receiver is appointed under a floating charge debenture, he is called an administrative receiver. This chapter relates to administrative receivers.

The appointment of a receiver is of no effect unless it is accepted by the receiver before the end of the next business day. Acceptance must be in writing or confirmed in writing before seven days. A form LQ01 is required for each separate charge registered at Companies House over part of the property or all the company's assets. An administrative receiver must also publish notice of his or her appointment in the Gazette and in an appropriate newspaper.

The receiver may apply to court for directions in relation to any matter arising in connection with the performance of his function. The court can fix the receivers remuneration if asked to do so by the liquidator of the company. The receiver must make it clear, on each invoice and other paperwork, that a receiver has been appointed.

A receiver is personally liable on any contract entered into by him and even in relation to any contract of employment adopted by him, though he is entitled to indemnity out of the assets of the company.

Priority of debt in receivership

If an asset is subject to a fixed charge, the receiver need have regard to no debts in priority to those owed to the fixed charge holder. If assets are subject only to a floating charge, then the receiver must ensure that the preferential creditors of the company are paid in full before the debenture holder receives any payment. Preferential creditors are defined in schedule 6 of the Act. If there is a surplus from the sale of a fixed charge asset after paying off the amount due to the charge, the surplus must not be used for the payment of preferential creditors but handed on to any liquidator subsequently appointed.

Powers of the receiver

The powers confirmed on a receiver are set out in schedule 1 to the Act and include the right to take or defend proceedings in the company's name, sell the company's assets, borrow money, appoint solicitors, use the company seal, carry on business and even petition for the winding up of the company. The receiver has power to apply to court to allow the disposal of an asset subject to a fixed charge as if that asset were not subject to such security. This is in order to prevent a creditor owed more than the value of his security preventing beneficial realisation of the company's assets. An English receiver's powers extend to assets in Scotland and vice versa.

Duties of a receiver

The receiver is under an obligation to notify the company and advertise notice of his appointment and within 28 days to send a similar notice to all creditors of the company. Every receiver or manager of a company's property must deliver to the Registrar of Companies an account of his receipts and payments every twelve months. An administrative receiver must report to creditors within three months after his appointment and send to the Registrar of Companies and all creditors a report of the events leading to his appointment, details of what property is being disposed by him, the amount owed to the debenture holders and to preferential creditors and the amount, if any, likely to be available to ordinary creditors. A copy of his report must also be given to a meeting of the company's ordinary creditors within the same time-scale.

The meeting of the creditors can decide to establish a committee "to assist the receiver". The committee can require a receiver to attend meetings and to provide it with information. The rules governing the above are to found in s46-49. The rules governing the conduct of the creditors meeting in a receivership are contained in rr3.9-3.15. The functions of the creditors committee are to assist the receiver and to act as agreed with him.

Statement of affairs

After an administrative receiver has been appointed, the directors of the company are under an obligation to submit a statement of affairs (s47). The statement should be in form 3.2 in schedule 4 to the rules and must be verified by affidavit. The court can order limited disclosure of the information contained in the statement of affairs or even release the directors from the obligation to submit such a statement.

VAT

No formalities are required to reclaim the VAT element of the debt owed by the bankrupt-the creditor is automatically entitled to VAT bad debt relief once he has written off the debt in his books and the debt is more than six months old.

Which forms should be used?

Following the implementation of the Insolvency Rules 2010, which came into force on 6th April 2010, Companies House will prescribe the following insolvency forms within Registrar's Rules. The forms listed below are to be filed with the Registrar for all receiverships.

Form	title no
Notice of the appointment of receiver or manager	LQ01
Notice of ceasing to act as receiver or manager	LQ02
Statement of affairs in administrative receivership	
Following report to creditors	3.3
Certificate of constitution of creditors committee	3.4
Administrative receivers report as to	

Chapter 11

Company Voluntary Arrangements

Nature of a Company Arrangement (CVA)

A CVA is an agreement between a company and its shareholders and creditors. There is little court involvement. It is only necessary for copies of certain documents to be lodged at court so as to be available for public inspection. Only an authorised insolvency practitioner may be the nominee and supervisor in a CVA. A CVA can be proposed even after a company has gone into administration or liquidation. The object of a CVA can either be a moratorium (a delay of payment until a certain event happens or payment by instalment) or the payment of less than 100p in the pound in full settlement.

The directors of a company, the liquidator or administrator can make a proposal for a CVA (S1). The proposal must contain an explanation why a CVA is desirable and why the company's creditors might be expected to agree with it, the proposal must set out details of the company's assets and liabilities, how it is proposed to deal with secured and preferential creditors and creditors who are connected to the company, whether there are any circumstances that might give rise to an adjustment of prior transactions, what costs were involved in the CVA, what duties the supervisors will undertake and so on.

If it is the directors who are putting forward the proposal, they must select an authorised insolvency practitioner to act as nominee. It is the nominees duty to report to the creditors (and to the court) on the directors proposal (r17). The proposers of the proposal must give to the nominee a statement of affairs relating to the company (r1.5) and all these documents must be lodged in court. If the nominee is of the opinion that there is some prospect of the CVA being approved, he will state that in his opinion a meeting of the shareholders and the creditors of the company should be convened to consider the proposal.

Meetings of shareholders and creditors

For a CVA to be approved, shareholders and creditors must give their approval. The shareholders meeting must be held on the same day but after creditors meeting . The rules as to the conduct of the meeting are contained in rr 1.14-16. For a CVA to be approved, there has to be a 75% majority in favour of it. The majority is calculated by reference to the value of the creditor's claim of those creditors present in person or by proxy and voting at the meeting. Shareholder's approval is given by simple majority.

If any shareholder or creditor feels that the meetings have not been conducted in accordance with the rules or that the interests of a shareholder or member have been unfairly prejudiced by the CVA, he may apply to the court for revocation or suspension of the CVA (s6). The court can order further meetings to be held. An approved CVA binds everyone who was given notice of, and was entitled to vote at, the meeting to consider the proposal whether or not he was actually present at the meeting. If the company is in administration or liquidation, the court may stay the proceedings and give directions with regard to the proceedings as are appropriate for facilitating the implementation of the CVA (s5 (3)). The winding up of the company is, however, not rescinded or reversed but simply stayed. The person whose function it is to carry out the CVA is the supervisor. He may apply to the court for directions in relation to any matters arising in the CVA and also to wind up the company if necessary.

Once a CVA is approved, the directors must do everything that is required for putting the supervisor into possession of the assets included in the arrangement. The supervisor has an obligation to keep accounts and records of his dealings and to prepare an account of all his receipts and payments not less than once every twelve months and send it to the courts, the registrar of companies, shareholders and creditors. The supervisor must also produce to the Secretary of State his records and accounts if so requested. Not more than 28 days after the final completion of the CVA the supervisor must send to all shareholders and creditors a notice that the CVA has been fully implemented, and lodge a copy with the court.

Chapter 12

The Administration Process

___

Nature of Administration

The current law concerning administration was introduced with effect from 15th September 2003. Under this regime, a company will usually be described as 'being in administration' – prior to this, a company would be described as being subject to an 'administration order'. Administrations were introduced into insolvency legislation to enable those appointed as administrator to run the business as a going concern, and promote the rehabilitation of that business. The objective of administration is to:

- ensure the survival of the company or in part as a going concern;
- achieve a better price for the company's assets or other wise realise their value more favourably for the creditors as a whole than would be likely if the company were wound up (without first being in administration; or
- in certain circumstances realise the value of that property in order to make a distribution to one or more preferential creditors.

How does a company enter administration?
A company enters administration when the appointment of an administrator takes effect. An administrator may be appointed by:

a) an administration order made by the court;
b) the holder of a floating charge;
c) The company or its directors.

The administrator must perform his or her functions as quickly or efficiently as is reasonably practical.

What are the effects on a company of being in administration?

When a company enters administration:

- any pending winding-up petitions will be dismissed or suspended;
- there will be a moratorium on insolvency and other legal proceedings;
- if an administrative receiver has been appointed, he must vacate office;
- if a receiver of part of the company's property has been appointed, he must vacate office (if the administrator requires this).

As soon as is reasonably practicably, an administrator must send a notice of his or her appointment to the company and each of the creditors and also to the London Gazette. In addition, notice must be posted in a local newspaper. The administrator must also send notice of his appointment to the Registrar.

While a company is in administration, every document issued by the company or administrator must state the name of the administrator and that he or she is managing the affairs, business and property of the company.

The administrator will request a statement of the company's affairs from relevant people, i.e. an officer of the company. As soon as is practicable, and before the end of eight weeks after the company enters administration, the administrator must make a statement setting out proposals for achieving the purpose of the administration or explaining why they cannot be achieved. The proposals may include a voluntary arrangement or a compromise with creditors or members.

The statement setting out the proposals must be sent to:

- The Registrar of Companies;
- Every creditor of the company whose claim and address he is aware; and
- Every member of the company whose address he is aware.

Each copy of the proposals sent must be accompanied by an invitation to a creditors meeting. The business of the initial creditors meeting will be to approve (with or without modifications) the statement of proposals. Following the initial meeting, the administrator may:

- hold further creditors meetings;
- form a creditors committee; or
- deal with matters in correspondence between the administrators and creditors.

The administrator must notify any revisions to the proposals following the creditors meeting to members. Any decision taken at a creditors meeting must be reported to the Registrar of Companies.

When does administration end?

There are several ways in which administration ends. It can automatically end when the administrator's term of office expires. The appointment of an administrator expires after one year. This may be extended with the consent of the court or the creditors. Any extension must be notified to the Registrar.

An administrator appointed under a court order may apply to the court to end administration if he or she thinks that the purpose of administration cannot be achieved or the company should not have entered administration, or a creditors meeting requires the application. The court will discharge the administration order and the administrator must notify the Registrar.

An administrator appointed by the holders of a floating charge or by the company or its directors may end administration when the purpose of administration has been sufficiently achieved. The administrator must file the notice with the court and the registrar.

Administration may end on the application of a creditor to the court alleging an improper motive on the part of the person who appointed the administrator or applied to the court for an administration order. The administrator must send a copy of the order with the relevant form to the Registrar.

Administration may end and move into a creditor's voluntary winding-up. This can happen where the administrator thinks that each secured creditor is likely to be paid and a distribution will be made to unsecured creditors, if any. The administrator must notify the Registrar and the company will be wound up as if a resolution for voluntary winding up had been passed, on the day on which notice is registered with the Registrar.

Administration may end and move into dissolution. This can happen if the administrator thinks that a company has no property with which to make a distribution to its creditors. The administrator must send notice of this to the Registrar and the company will be dissolved after the date the form is registered.

Dissolution will occur after the three-month period unless an order is made to extend or suspend the period. Notice of the order must be notified to the Registrar.

The forms to use in administration

Following the implementation of the Insolvency (amendment) Rules 2010, which came into effect on 6th April 2010, Companies House will prescribe the following Insolvency forms within Registrar's rules for the first time. The forms listed below are to be filed with the Registrar, for all in administration. For any in administration that started on or before 5th April 2010 these forms may be used with appropriate amendments, if required.

See below
.

FORM	NUMBER
Notice of Administrator's appointment	2.12B (CH)
Notice of statement of affairs	2.16B
Statement of administrator's proposals	2.17B

Notice of extension of time period	2.18B (CH)
Notice of deemed approval of proposals	F2.18
Statement of administrator's revised proposals	2.22B (CH)
Notice of result of meeting of creditors	2.23B (CH)
Administrator's progress report	2.24B
(Amended) Certificate of Constitution of creditors committee	2.26B
Notice of order to deal with charged property	2.28B
Notice of automatic end to administration	2.30B
Notice of extension of period of administration	2.31B
Notice of end of administration	2.32(B)
Notice of court order ending administration	2.33B
Notice of move from administration to creditors voluntary liquidation	2.34B
Notice of move from administration to dissolution	2.35B
Notice to registrar of Companies with respect of date of dissolution	2.36B
Notice of intention to resign as	2.37B

administrator	
Notice of resignation by administrator	2.38B (CH)
Notice of vacation of office by administrator	2.39B
Notice of appointment of replacement/additional administrator	2.40B

These forms are not available to download from Companies House. Copies can be obtained from law stationers.

Chapter 13

Insolvent Partnerships

Definition of a partnership

A partnership is a relationship which exists between two or more persons carrying on business together with a view to making a profit. A partner can be an individual or a company (known as a corporate member) and is personally liable (usually without limit) for the debts of the partnership. Therefore a creditor of a partnership can pursue one or more of the partners personally, as well as the partnership itself, for a partnership debt.

Winding up a partnership that owes money

Because the partners are personally liable for the debts of the partnership, a partnership can be wound up and bankruptcy orders can also be made against the individual partners..

If you are a creditor of a partnership, you can apply for either:

1. the winding up of the insolvent partnership as an unregistered company with no action taken against the individual partners (under Article 7 of the Insolvent Partnerships Order 1994); or

2. the winding up of the insolvent partnership as an unregistered company where bankruptcy petitions are also presented against one or more of the partners (under Article 8 of the Insolvent Partnerships Order 1994).

A creditor can only apply for a winding-up order against the partnership if the partnership has traded in England or Wales at any time in the 3 years before the petition is presented.

As the partners are personally liable for the debts of the partnership, a creditor of a partnership can petition (apply) for the bankruptcy of one or more of the partners, without petitioning for the partnership to be wound up. More information on presenting a bankruptcy petition can be obtained from the Insolvency Service site www.insolvency.gov.uk

The leaflet "Dealing with Debt: How to make someone bankrupt" deals with petitioning an individual whilst "Dealing with debt: How to wind up a company that owes you money" deals with a corporate member.

Winding up your own partnership

The partnership can either:

1. petition for the winding up of the partnership as an unregistered company with no bankruptcy petitions presented against the individual partners (under Article 9 of the Insolvent Partnerships Order 1994): or

2. petition for the winding up of the partnership as an unregistered company where bankruptcy petitions are also presented against all the individual partners (under Article 10 of the Insolvent Partnerships Order 1994): or

3. petition for bankruptcy orders to be made against all the partners (known as a Form 16 petition under Article 11 of the Insolvent Partnerships Order 1994). The petition must be presented jointly by all the partners. It can only be presented where all the partners are individuals. If one or more of the partners is a corporate member, the petition must be presented under article 10 of the Insolvent Partnerships Order 1994 (as above). A formal winding-up order is not made against the partnership, but any order made as a result of a Form 16 petition will include authority for the partnership to be wound up by the trustee appointed to deal with the bankrupt partners affairs.

If a bankruptcy petition has already been presented against one of the partners, and the court is made aware of the insolvent partnership, the court may make an order regarding how the partnership affairs should be dealt with.

As the partners are personally liable for the debts of the partnership, an individual partner can apply for his or her bankruptcy without applying for the partnership to be wound up. The Insolvency Service website has a leaflet "Dealing with debt: How to petition for your own bankruptcy" which outlines how to go about this.

What happens after a partnership is wound up?

Where a winding-up order has been made against the partnership, the partnership affairs are dealt with in the same way as a limited company.

Chapter 14

Deceased Insolvents

The provisions for dealing with a deceased debtor

It is often thought that when a person dies, his/her debts are automatically discharged. However, this is a misconception. Debts are *not* discharged on death unless specific provision has been made for them to be discharged, e.g. by an insurance policy. All debts that are not provided for must be met from the assets of the deceased debtor. Where the assets are insufficient to meet all the debts, then the estate is insolvent.

Where a person dies *after* a bankruptcy petition is presented against him/her, the matter continues as a normal bankruptcy with some amendments. Where a person dies *before* a bankruptcy petition is presented, a petition for an insolvency administration order can be presented under the Administration of Insolvent Estates of Deceased Persons Order 1986 (AIEDPO86). The administration of the insolvent estate is dealt with under the provisions of the AIEDPO86, which applies and amends certain provisions of the Insolvency Act 1986.

Who can present a petition for an insolvency administration order?

Where a person dies before a bankruptcy petition has been presented, a petition for an insolvency administration order can be presented to the court by a creditor or creditors jointly, the deceased's personal representative, a temporary administrator, a liquidator appointed in proceedings by virtue of Article 3(1) of the EC Regulation on Insolvency Proceedings, where the deceased entered into a voluntary arrangement, the supervisor of that arrangement or a creditor bound by it, the official petitioner, where the deceased person was subject to a criminal bankruptcy order.

Where the petition is presented by a creditor or personal representative the court must be shown that it is reasonably probable that the estate is insolvent before an insolvency administration order will be granted.

Between the presentation of the petition and the making of an insolvency administration order, the court may appoint the official receiver as interim receiver to protect the assets. The official receiver's duties may be restricted so care should be taken to ensure any restrictions are observed. Otherwise, the official receiver as interim receiver has all the powers and duties of a receiver and manager. The personal representative has a duty to co-operate with the interim receiver and to provide details of the assets which should be taken into immediate possession pending the hearing of the petition.

Who should the official receiver contact for information on the insolvent estate after an insolvency administration order is made?

On receipt of an insolvency administration order, the official receiver should contact the deceased debtor's personal representative as soon as possible. The personal representative is either the person named as executor in the deceased debtor's will with the responsibility of administering the estate of the deceased, or where the deceased debtor died without making a will (intestate), a person who is known as the administrator, who is granted letters of administration by a court of probate. A search to establish whether a grant of representation has been issued can be carried out by completing the probate search form PA1S (which can be found at http://www.hmcourts-service.gov.uk/ under "forms and guidance") and sending it to:

The Postal Searches & Copies Department
York Probate Sub-Registry
Castle Chambers
Clifford Street
York
YO1 9RG

A fee of £6 is payable for a search to be carried out, which covers the four-year period from the date of death. There is an additional fee of £4 for each subsequent four-year period searched. If a grant is traced, the fee includes a copy of the grant, and a copy of the will if there is one. Cheques should be made payable to "HM Paymaster General". (fees correct as at 2012)

A grant cannot be located without at least the correct full name of the deceased debtor, and the year from which the search is to begin. The Probate Service aims to supply copies of documents within 21 working days of receipt of an application.

Where there is no personal representative or administrator, the official receiver should contact the closest surviving relative of the deceased debtor. Where this Part refers to personal representative, it should be taken as meaning the personal representative, administrator or closest surviving relative as applicable.

The personal representative may be a professional person, such as a solicitor, or a relative of the deceased debtor. Where the personal representative is a relative, the official receiver should be sensitive in dealing with him/her to avoid adding to the natural distress he/she may be feeling.

A statement of affairs must be submitted to the official receiver within 56 days of the insolvency administration order being made. The personal representative is required to complete this, or, in the absence of a personal representative, such other person as the court may direct. The statement of affairs should contain both the position at the date of death and at the making of the insolvency administration order, and should be completed on the statutory form SADI.

What are the personal representative's duties in relation to the official receiver?

The personal representative has similar duties to that of a bankrupt in a bankruptcy. As well as the duty to submit a statement of affairs, he/she must notify the official receiver of any assets which may be claimed for the estate by the trustee, provide an inventory of the estate to the official receiver, attend on the official receiver as reasonably required, and provide information regarding the assets, liabilities and affairs of the deceased debtor. If the personal representative fails to comply with his/her obligations he/she may be guilty of a contempt of court, and the official receiver may apply for him/her to be privately examined if he/she will not comply with his/her obligations voluntarily.

The official receiver becomes receiver and manager when the insolvency administration order is made, and control of the estate is removed from the personal representative on that date.

Some protection is afforded to the personal representative regarding asset disposals made between the presentation of a petition for an insolvency administration order and the date of the order so long as the disposal was carried out in good faith. It is probable that good faith means without notice of the petition or without awareness of the insolvency of the deceased debtor.

Where the personal representative has notice of the petition, he/she is restrained from disposing of any of the assets of the estate. If the official receiver becomes aware that such a disposal has been made by the personal representative after notice of the petition, and it has not been subsequently ratified by the court, he/she should immediately write to the person to whom the payment has been made or the asset been transferred, requiring them to hold the monies or property to the order of the official receiver for the benefit of the insolvent estate.

What should the official receiver do once he/she is notified of an insolvency administration order?

Notices similar to those issued on the making of a bankruptcy order should be sent out. All notices sent out should be headed "In the matter of the Administration of Insolvent Estates of Deceased Persons Order 1986", and should refer to an insolvency administration order and the deceased debtor.

The deceased debtor must not be referred to as a bankrupt and the terms "bankruptcy" and "bankruptcy order" must not be used. The official receiver should contact the deceased debtor's personal representative immediately using form NPRDD (notice to personal representative of deceased debtor), and enclosing a statement of affairs form SADI (statement of affairs for deceased insolvent) for completion by the personal representative, who should also be asked to provide a copy of the death certificate and a copy of the last will made by the deceased debtor prior to his/her death.

It will not usually be necessary to ask the personal representative to complete a preliminary information questionnaire B40.01/PIQB. If more information is needed in addition to that contained in the statement of affairs, it will generally be more appropriate for the official receiver to ask the personal representative further questions as necessary.

If there are sufficient assets to warrant the appointment of an insolvency practitioner as trustee, the official receiver should call a meeting of creditors in the usual way. All notices and forms sent should be amended to make it clear that the meeting relates to the insolvency administration order and not to a bankruptcy order. The proof of debt forms should show the date of death as being the date to which claims should be made.

What are the official receivers duties in respect of an insolvency administration order?

The official receiver has the normal duties of a receiver and manager or trustee in bankruptcy. In addition, if the official receiver is trustee, he/she must have regard to any claim made by the personal representative in respect of reasonable funeral, testamentary and administrative expenses incurred. These claims have priority over the preferential debts, but are only payable from the estate balance if it is in credit after all administrative expenses of the insolvency administration order have been paid. The official receiver should take account of such a claim before making any distribution to creditors.

As trustee, the official receiver's title to the assets dates back to the date of death as if the presentation of the petition, the insolvency administration order and the death all took place on the same day. A deceased debtor's share in property held on a joint tenancy does not form part of his/her estate which passes under his/her will or intestacy; it passes by survivorship to the surviving joint tenant. Because of the right of survivorship when an insolvency administration order is made, the deceased debtor's interest in jointly held assets, such as a balance in a jointly held bank account, will pass to the surviving partner. The deceased debtor's interest in jointly held assets (other than those held under a tenancy in common) will not fall within the estate.

The official receiver has no statutory duty to investigate the affairs of the deceased debtor unless he/she thinks fit.

What happens to property that was owned under a joint tenancy by the deceased debtor prior to his/her death?

The deceased debtor's interest in property owned under a joint tenancy will pass automatically to the other joint owner or owners by right of survivorship, and will never become part of the insolvency estate.

The trustee may seek to recover the value of the deceased debtor's interest in the property that has been lost to the estate by making an application to the court under section 421A. On the application of the trustee the court may make an order requiring the surviving partner to pay to the trustee an amount not exceeding the value lost to the estate. Section 421A came into force on 02 April 2001 and applies where an insolvency administration order has been made in respect of the deceased debtor and the petition for that order was presented within the period of five years beginning on the day on which he/she died.

What happens to property that was owned under a tenancy in common or solely by the deceased debtor prior to his/her death?

Where the deceased debtor's sole or principal residence is owned solely by the deceased debtor or is jointly owned under a tenancy in common the provisions of section 283A may apply. Section 283A was introduced by the Enterprise Act 2002 and provides that the interest in such a dwelling-house will re-vest in the bankrupt 3 years from the date of the bankruptcy order (or 3 years from the date the official receiver or other trustee becomes aware of its existence) without conveyance, assignment or transfer unless the trustee has taken action to dispose or otherwise deal with the bankrupt's interest in it. AIEDPO86 Schedule 1 Part II paragraph 12 adopts sections 283 to 285 and current legal advice is that this includes section 283A but no provision is contained in the legislation to modify the language of section 283A in order to apply to the estate of a deceased debtor. An amendment to the AIEDPO86 may be made in the future to clarify this position.

In the meantime the official receiver should assume that section 283A does apply and in the case of a deceased debtor with a solely owned property or a tenancy in common in a dwelling house, the interest in the dwelling house would vest in the personal representatives of the deceased (or such person as the court may order) if the trustee took no action within 3 years. The official receiver should therefore take all necessary steps to realise his/her interest in the property within the three-year period (starting at the date of death) in order to avoid a later claim that the property ceases to be comprised in the insolvency estate by virtue of section 283A.

What happens when a debtor dies after a bankruptcy petition is presented?

When a debtor dies after a bankruptcy petition is presented the proceedings will continue as normal, and if an order is made by the court it is a bankruptcy order and is administered accordingly, with some necessary modifications. The deceased debtor's personal representative or other appropriate person is required to complete a statement of affairs. The reasonable funeral and testamentary expenses have priority over the preferential debts, whether the deceased debtor dies before or after the making of the bankruptcy order.

Where a deceased debtor owned property under a joint tenancy and died after a bankruptcy petition was presented but before a bankruptcy order was made, the deceased debtor's interest in the property passes to the surviving tenant and does not form part of the estate. Section 421A does not apply in this case, and the value lost to the estate cannot be recovered.

Glossary of terms

Administration order-this is an order made in a county court to arrange and administer the payment of debts by an individual.

Annulment-cancellation.

Assets-anything that belongs to a debtor that may be used to pay off debts.

Bankrupt-a person against whom a bankruptcy order has been made by a court.

Bankruptcy-the process of dealing with the estate of a bankrupt

Bankruptcy restriction notice-a notice entered at the Land Registry on any property involved in a bankruptcy.

Bankruptcy order-a court order making an individual bankrupt.

Bankruptcy petition- a request made to the court for a debtor to be made bankrupt.

Bankruptcy restrictions order or undertaking- a procedure whereby the restrictions of bankruptcy continue to apply for between 2-15 years.

Charging order- an order made by the court giving the trustee a legal charge on the bankrupt's property for the amount owed.

Creditor-someone who is owed money by a bankrupt.

Creditor's committee- a committee representing the interests of all creditors in supervising the activities of a trustee in bankruptcy.

Debt Management Plan-an informal arrangement negotiated with creditors by an independent company.

Debt Relief Order-an alternative to bankruptcy for smaller debts.

Debtor-someone who owes money.

Discharge-free from bankruptcy.

Estate-assets or property of the bankrupt which the trustee can use to pay creditors.

Fast Track Voluntary Arrangement-a voluntary agreement with creditors to pay all or part of the money owed, which can only be entered into when bankrupt.

Income payment agreements (IPA) a written agreement where the bankrupt voluntarily agrees to pay the trustee part of his or her income for an agreed period.

Income payments order (IPO)-where the court orders the bankrupt to pay part of their income to the trustee for a period.

Individual Voluntary Arrangement (IVA)-a voluntary arrangement for an individual where a compromise scheme for payment of debts is put to creditors.
Insolvency-being unable to pay debts when they are due.

Insolvency practitioner-an authorised person specialising in insolvency, usually a solicitor or accountant.

Nominee-an insolvency practitioner who carries out the preparatory work for a voluntary arrangement.

Non-provable debt-debt which is not included in the bankruptcy proceedings. An individual remains liable for such debt regardless of his or her bankruptcy.

Official receiver-a civil servant and officer of the court employed by the Insolvency Service, which deals with bankruptcies.

Petition-a formal application made to court by the debtor or creditor.

Preferential creditor-a creditor entitled to receive certain payments in priority to other unsecured creditors.

Public examination-where the Official receiver questions the bankrupt in open court.

Secured creditor-a creditor holding security, such as a mortgage.

Secured creditor-a charge or mortgage over assets taken to secure the payment of a debt. Where the debt is not paid, the lender has the right to sell the charged assets.

Statement of affairs-a document completed by a bankrupt and sworn under oath, stating the assets and giving details of debtors and creditors.

Trustee-either the Official Receiver or an insolvency practitioner who takes control over the assets of a bankrupt.

Unsecured creditor-a creditor who does not hold any security for money owed.

Unsecured debt-a debt owed to an unsecured creditor.

Useful Addresses and Websites

The Bankruptcy Association
Free Post L A 1118
4 Johnson Close
Lancaster
LA1 5BR
Tel: 01539 469474
Email: johnmcqueen@thba.org.uk
www.theba.org.uk

Her Majesty's Court Services (hmcs)
Lewins Place
Lewins Mead
Bristol
BS1 2NR
Bankruptcy Section
Tel: 0117 910 6726   or 0117 910 6756
Email: enquiries@bristol.countycourt.gsi.gov.uk
www.hmcourt-service.gov.uk

(Bankruptcy Information Centre)
Birkenhead County Bankruptcy Court Information
76 Hamilton Street
Birkenhead
Merseyside
CH41 5EN
Tel: 0151 666 5800

enquiries@birkenhead.countycourt.gsi.gov.uk
bankruptcy.org.uk/423/bankruptcy-courts/birkenhead-cou

Debt Management, Debt Consolidation, IVA, Bankruptcy, Trust Deeds.

4th Floor
The Chancery
58 Spring Gardens
Manchester
M2 1EW1
Freephone: 0800 228 9288
www.chasesaunders.co.uk

Insolvency Service

www. bis.gov.uk/insolvency
0845 602 9848

Insolvency Practitioners

Griffin and King
26-28 Goodall Street
Walsall
West Midlands
WS1 1QL
Tel: 01922 722205
www.griffinandking.co.uk
Email: enquiries@griffinandking.co.uk
Their Bournemouth Office
10 Poole Hill
Bournemouth
Dorset
BH2 5PS
Tel: 01202 355348

Their Shewsbury Office

9 Hotspur Street
Shewsbury
SY1 2PZ
Tel: 01743 491239
Email your enquiries to their Licensed Insolvency Practitioners
Tim Corfield at tim@griffinandking.co.uk
Or Janet Peacock at janet.peacock@griffinandking.co.uk

Ward & Co Insolvency Practitioners
Bank House
7 Shaw Street
Worcester
WR1 3QQ
Tel: 0845 263354
www.companyliquidationworcester.co.uk

Debtsolver
Trafford Plaza
73 Seymour Grove
Manchaster
M16 OLD
Tel: 08000 434 336
Email: info@debtsolver.co.uk
www.debtsolver.co.uk

Bankruptcy Information
Alton Chambers
37 Church Road
Poole
Dorset
BH14 8UF
Tel: 01202 714868 or

0800 5977 977
www.bankruptcy.co.uk

Citizens Advice Bureau
Helpline 0207 833 2181
www.citizensadvice.org.uk

Community Legal Services
Helpline 0845 345 4345
www.clsdirect.org.uk

Consumer Credit Counselling Service
The CCCS is a registered charity dedicated to providing free, confidential counselling and money management help to families and individuals in financial distress

Helpline 0800 138 1111
www.cccs.co.uk

Consumer Direct
Consumer Direct is the government funded telephone and online service offering information and advice on consumer issues.
Helpline 0845 404 0506
www.consumerdirect.gov.uk

National Debtline
National Debtline provides free confidential and independent advice over the telephone for anyone in financial difficulties.

Helpline 0808 808 4000
www.nationaldebtline.co.uk

Index

L
Law Society, 32
Licensed Insolvency Practitioners, 21, 125
Life insurance policy, 54
Loans, 33

M
Making payments, 18

N
Non-provable debts, 49

O
Official Receiver, 3, 11, 12, 13, 36, 37, 38, 45, 47, 48, 49, 50, 51, 52, 53, 56, 58, 122
Overdrafts, 15, 33

P
Payments to creditors, 49
Pension rights, 54
Personal loans, 15
Preferential debts, 50

R
Registry of County Court Judgements, 30
Rent, 33
Restrictions on a bankrupt, 55

S
Secured borrowing, 15
Social fund loans, 33
Store cards, 15

Appendix 1 Useful forms

1. Petition for Bankruptcy

2. Petition for company winding up

Debtor's Bankruptcy Petition
(Title)

(a) Insert full name, address and occupation (if any) of debtor

I

(a)_____

_____

_____

(b) Insert in full any other name(s) by which the debtor is or has been known

also known as

(b)_____

(c) Insert former address or addresses at which the debtor may have incurred debts or liabilities still unpaid or unsatisfied

[lately residing at

(c)_____

_____

(d) Insert trading name (adding "with another or others", if this is so), business address and nature of the business

[and carrying on business as (d) _____

_____

_____]

(e) Insert any former trading names (adding "with another or others", if this is so), business address and nature of the business in respect of which the debtor may have incurred debts or liabilities still unpaid or unsatisfied

[and lately carrying on business as (e) _____

_____

_____

_____

_____]

request the court that a bankruptcy order be made against me and say as follows:-

(f) Delete as applicable

1. (f) [My centre of main interests is in England and Wales][I have an establishment in England and Wales.]

OR

I carry on business as an insurance undertaking; a credit institution; investment undertaking providing services involving the holding of funds or securities for third parties; or a collective investment undertaking as referred to in Article 1.2 of the EC Regulation.

OR

My centre of main interests is not within a Member State

Under the EC Regulation
(i) Centre of main interests should correspond to the place where the debtor conducts the administration of his interests on a regular basis.
(ii) Establishment is defined in the Council Regulation (No 1346/2000) on insolvency proceedings as "any place of operations where the debtor caries out a non-transitory economic activity with human means and goods"

2. I am (f)[not] resident in England and Wales. I am presenting this petition to the High Court because (f)[I have neither carried on business nor resided in England and Wales within the 6 months immediately preceding the presentation of this petition][I am a member of an insolvent partnership (f)[which is being wound up][in relation to which a winding-up petition has been presented which has not yet been disposed of]].

OR

I am (f)[not] resident in England and Wales. I am presenting this petition to the (f)[High Court][Central London County Court] because (f)[I carried on business in England and Wales within the 6 months immediately preceding the presentation of this petition and I carried on business within the area of the London insolvency district (f)[for the greater part of that period of 6 months][for a longer period than in any other insolvency district]][I have not carried on business in England and Wales but have resided in England and Wales within the 6 months immediately preceding the presentation of this petition and I resided within the area of the London insolvency district (f)[for the greater part of that period of 6 months][for a longer period than in any other insolvency district]] and the unsecured liabilities set out in the statement of affairs attached to this petition are (f)[£100,000 or more][less than £100,000].

OR

I am (f)[not] resident in England and Wales. I am presenting this petition to this county court because within the 6 months immediately preceding the presentation of this petition (f)[I carried on business in England and Wales and for the longest part of the period during which I carried on business in England and Wales within that 6 period of months, the (f)[principal] place of business was situated in the district of (f)[this][..........] county court][I have not carried on business in England and Wales but resided in England and Wales and for the longest part of the period during which I resided in England and Wales within that period of 6 months, I resided in the district of (f)[this][............] county court]][and in order to expedite the presentation of this petition, I am presenting it to this court as it is the [nearest full time] court (f)[to my [principal] place of business][for the insolvency district in which I reside]].

3. I am unable to pay my debts.

4. (f) That within the period of five years ending with the date of this petition:-

(j) Insert date

(i) I have not been adjudged bankrupt

(k) Insert name of court

OR

I was adjudged bankrupt on (j)   in the (k)

(l) Insert number of bankruptcy proceedings

Court No. (l)

(ii) I have not (f) [made a composition with my creditors in satisfaction of my debts] or (f) [entered into a scheme of arrangement with creditors] (S16 BA1914)

OR

On (j)   I (f) [made a composition] [entered into a scheme of arrangement] with my creditors.

(iii) I have not entered into a voluntary arrangement

OR

On (j)   I entered into a voluntary arrangement

(iv) I have not been subject to an administration order under Part VI of the County Courts Act 1984

OR

On (j)   an administration order was made against me in the
(l)   county court.

5. A statement of my affairs is filed with this petition.

Date_____

Signature_____

Complete only if petition not heard immediately

Endorsement
This petition having been presented to the court on _____ it is ordered that the petition shall be heard as follows:-
Date _____
Time _____ hours
Place_____

Rule 4.7   Form 4.2
                    Winding-Up Petition

                (Title)   (Registered No.   )

(a) Insert title of court   To (a)

(b) Insert full name(s)   The petition of (b)
and address(es) of
petitioner(s)

(c) Insert full name   1. (c)
and registered no. of
company subject to
petition
                             (hereinafter called "the company") was incorporated on

(d) Insert date of   (d)
incorporation

                             under the Companies Act 19

(e) Insert address of   2. The registered office of the company is at (e)
registered office

(f) Insert amount of   3. The nominal capital of the company is (f) £
nominal capital and
how it is divided   divided into   shares of £   each. The amount of the capital paid up or credited
(g) Insert amount of   as paid up is (g) £
capital paid up or
credited as paid up

                             4. The principal objects for which the company was established are as follows:

                             and other objects stated in the memorandum of association of the company

(h) Set out the   5. (h)
grounds on which a
winding-up order is
sought

(j) Delete as   6. The company (j) is/is not an insurance undertaking; a credit institution; an investment
applicable   undertaking providing services involving the holding of funds or securities for third
                             parties; or a collective investment undertaking as referred to in Article 1.2 of the EC
                             Regulation.

(k) Insert name of   7. For the reasons stated in the statement of truth of (k)   filed in
person making the   support here of it is considered that the EC Regulation on insolvency proceedings (j)
statement of truth   will/will not apply (j) and that these proceedings will be (l)_____
(l) Insert whether   proceedings as defined in Article 3 of the EC Regulation
main, secondary or
territorial proceedings   (7A) (j)[A statutory demand was served on the company on (ll). More than 4 months
                             have elapsed between the service of the statutory demand and the presentation of this
(ll) Insert date of   petition for the reasons set out in the statement of truth of (k)
service   filed in support hereof.]

8. In the circumstances it is just and equitable that the company should be wound up
The petitioner(s) therefore pray(s) as follows:-

(1) that (c)

may be wound up by the court under the provisions of the Insolvency Act 1986
or
(2) that such other order may be made as the court thinks fit

(m) If the company is the petitioner, delete "the company". Add the full name and address of any other person on whom it is intended to serve this petition

Note: It is intended to serve this petition on (m)
[the company] [and]

Endorsement

This petition having been presented to the court
on _____ will be heard at (n) [Royal Courts of Justice, Strand,

(n) Insert name and address of Court

London, WC2A 2LL] [(n) _____ County Court
_____]

(o) Insert name and address of District Registry

[(o) _____ District Registry
_____]

on:

Date_____

Time _____hours
(or as soon thereafter as the petition can be heard)

The solicitor to the petitioner is:-

Name_____

Address_____

_____

Telephone no_____

Reference_____

(j) [Whose London Agents are:-

Name_____

Address_____

_____

Telephone no. _____

Reference_____

www.straightforwardco.co.uk
All titles, listed below, in the Straightforward Guides Series can be purchased online, using credit card or other forms of payment by going to www.straightfowardco.co.uk A discount of 25% per title is offered with online purchases.

Law
A Straightforward Guide to:
Consumer Rights
Bankruptcy Insolvency and the Law
Employment Law
Private Tenants Rights
Family law
Small Claims in the County Court
Contract law
Intellectual Property and the law
Divorce and the law
Leaseholders Rights
The Process of Conveyancing
Knowing Your Rights and Using the Courts
Producing Your own Will
Housing Rights
The Bailiff the law and You
Probate and The Law
Company law
What to Expect When You Go to Court
Guide to Competition Law
Give me Your Money-Guide to Effective Debt Collection
Caring for a Disabled Child

General titles
Letting Property for Profit
Buying, Selling and Renting property
Buying a Home in England and France
Bookkeeping and Accounts for Small Business
Creative Writing
Freelance Writing
Writing Your own Life Story
Writing performance Poetry
Writing Romantic Fiction
Speech Writing
Teaching Your Child to Read and write
Teaching Your Child to Swim
Raising a Child-The Early Years
Creating a Successful Commercial Website
The Straightforward Business Plan
The Straightforward C.V.
Successful Public Speaking
Handling Bereavement
Play the Game-A Compendium of Rules
Individual and Personal Finance
Understanding Mental Illness
The Two Minute Message
Guide to Self Defence

Go to:

www.straightforwardco.co.uk